www.HowToPutYourWholeSelfIn.com

# How to *Put Your* Whole *Self In*

## **101** Instructions on Becoming Good for Yourself, Good for Others, & Good for Heaven's Sake

# DR. DONALD HUNTINGTON

How To Put Your Whole Self In
101 Days to Become Good for Myself, Good for Others,
and Good for Heaven's Sake

Dr. Donald Huntington

ISBN-13: 978-1463750541
ISBN-10: 1463750544

First Edition
September 2011

Book design Patricia Hamilton
Cover design Adam Huntington

Published by
Park Place Publications
P.O. Box 829
Pacific Grove, CA 93950
www.parkplacepublications.com

Printed in United States of America

# Contents

Dedication                                    9
Acknowledgements                             11
Foreword                                     13
Introduction                                 15

## Part I—Become a Helpful Person and a Source of Blessing

Day 1—Give Yourself the Gift of Living Well            18
Day 2—Lead an Elevated Life                            20
Day 3—Be a Good Egg                                    22
Day 4—Leave Errors Alone                               24
Day 5—Put Away Fearfulness                             26
Day 6—Don't Fret About Things Like Death and Cancer    28
Day 7—Remain Busy with Happy Activities                30
Day 8—Kick Bad Habits                                  32
Day 9—Find People Beautiful                            34
Day 10—Rejoice in Working                              36
Day 11—Cultivate Hopeful Humility                      38
Day 12—Remain Connected to the Source                  40
Day 13—Follow the Path of Integrity                    42
Day 14—Stand Against Gossip                            44
Day 15—Put into Practice Einstein's Other Formula      46
Day 16—Look for the Good; Accentuate the Positive      48
Day 17—Listen Up!                                      50
Day 18—Find Your Purpose                               52
Day 19—Dance to the Rhythms                            54
Day 20—Walk in Forgiveness                             56
Day 21—Be Excellent Towards Yourself and Others        58

Day 22—Focus on the Present 60

Day 23—Move into a Sun-filled Space 62

Day 24—Learn to Boost Others 64

Day 25—Make Blessings Count 66

Day 26—Set the Course of Your Life 68

Day 27—Keep Calm in the Middle of Storms 70

Day 28—Embrace the Future with Anticipation and Delight 72

Day 29—Hold on to Your Opinions with a Light Grip 74

Day 30—Love Your Way into Health 76

Day 31—Become Habitually Excellent 78

Day 32—Sing a Song of Silence 80

Day 33—Think No Evil 82

## Part II—Learn Practical Truths and Bits of Wisdom

Day 34—Connect with the Source of Your Power 86

Day 35—Open Your Mind and Heart 88

Day 36—Embrace Sunrises and the Laughter of Children 90

Day 37—Bask in the Pink of Health; the Best of Times 92

Day 38—Realize That it Really Is a Wonderful Life 94

Day 39—Avoid Cheap Pleasure 96

Day 40—Learn Unforced Rhythms of Work and Repose 98

Day 41—Take Two-minute Vacations 100

Day 42—Open Your Eyes to Surrounding Miracles 102

Day 43—Recycle Your Garbage 104

Day 44—Be a Potato 106

Day 45—Eliminate Negative Attitudes 108

Day 46—Keep Your Feet on an Upward Path 110

Day 47—Be Willing to Be Dazzled 112

Day 48—Regard Life as a Learning Center or Dance Studio 114

Day 49—Bury Your Hurts 116

Day 50—Take Your Stand on Giant Shoulders 118

Day 51—Minimize Religion 120

Day 52—Reflect Deeply Upon Life ................................ 122

Day 53—Get Rid of Old Nonsense ............................... 124

Day 54—Dance with Your Eyes Wide Open ................. 126

Day 55—Embrace Life as it Is ...................................... 128

Day 56—Don't Bother Preparing for Death ................. 130

Day 57—Understand That You Don't Understand Much ... 132

Day 58—Question Everything ........................................ 134

Day 59—Commit to Life-Long Learning ...................... 136

Day 60—Listen Meaning into Silence ........................... 138

Day 61—Expect Miracles .............................................. 140

Day 62—Embrace the Surprising Joy of Humility ........ 142

Day 63—Be Small Enough Each Night to go to Bed .... 144

Day 64—Don't Forgive Until You're Ready .................. 146

Day 65—Fearlessly Seek the Truth ............................... 148

## Part III—Practice Gracious Deeds and Behaviors

Day 66—Reach out to Beautiful Things ........................ 152

Day 67—Relate to Others for Mercy's Sake ................. 154

Day 68—Love the Mob     Day 69—Hug Your Way into Health ... 158

Day 70—Make Others Feel Great .................................. 160

Day 71—Don't Strike Back ............................................ 162

Day 72—Live Above Desperation .................................. 164

Day 73—Just Show Up ................................................... 166

Day 74—Fearlessly Engage in Life ................................ 168

Day 75—Let Others Spit on You .................................. 170

Day 76—Take Advantage of Reciprocating Generosity ... 172

Day 77—Lift People Up ................................................. 174

Day 78—Clean the Cheese off Your Mustache ............. 176

Day 79—Leave Other People's Crackers Alone ............. 178

Day 80—Do the Right Thing ........................................ 180

Day 81—Learn to Move and to Remain Immovable ..... 182

Day 82—Treat Yourself to the Greatest Happiness ....... 184

Day 83—Remain Engaged                                        186

Day 84—Engage Completely with Your Life Partner             188

Day 85—Manage Your Reflection                               190

Day 86—Operate out of Your Passions                         192

Day 87—Be Diligent in Your Work                             194

Day 88—Serve Others                                         196

Day 89—Practice Temperance                                  198

Day 90—Let Go of the Wrong Right                            200

Day 91—Practice Resignation                                 202

Day 92—Permit Yourself to Chill                             204

Day 93—Live Without Desperation                             206

Day 94—Listen for the Footsteps of God                      208

Day 95—Help Yourself                                        210

Day 96—Press On                                             212

Day 97—Keep Laughing                                        214

Day 98—Learn to "Just Deal with it"                         216

Day 99—Do a Little Bit of Good                              218

Day 100—Embrace Every Moment with Gusto                     220

Day 101—Prepare to Be Blessed for a Change                  222

# Dedication

*To Rae*
*My best critic, my best friend,*
*beloved counselor, comforter,*
*companion, lover, and wife.*

# Acknowledgements

I'm so grateful for the people who helped and encouraged me with this project. I'm especially thankful to Patricia Hamilton, my publisher, for the advice that she gave in every step of the process. I'm grateful to my wife Rae and Karen Lyles who edited the book.

Special thanks is due to David York, Cindy Scarborough, Fred Ehler, Dena Jeglum, Beth Rutherford, Tammy Mendoza, Brett Morey, and Sayra Flores for the hours each of them spent pouring through the manuscript pages and sending corrections and suggestions that added both polish and substance to the finished product. Special thanks also to my partner and friend, Patricia Piquero, for her unfailing support and encouragement. Kudos to Adam Huntington for help with the cover design. Most of all, I am thankful to Amanda Blanc for her generous service as my webmaster.

# Foreword

My own spirit was fired up when my friend Carolyn told me that she was going to begin to live life on purpose. I'm living on purpose myself and have written this book to assist you in living on purpose yourself. Using words from The Message Translation of the Bible, this book will help you to "Strip down, start running—and never quit!"

I am respectful (sometimes in awe of) the faith of people from all religious traditions. In the following pages, I have chosen to refer to the Higher Power as "The Master." Join me in acknowledging him as Jesus, if you wish, but feel free to make whatever translation you desire—God, Yahweh, Allah, Vishnu, The Great Spirit, or as a personification of life itself....

I am a devout follower of Jesus Christ, though not a particularly good Christian. However you picture it, the Ultimate Power behind the universe—which is both personal and benevolent—will lead you through life as long as you maintain the connection unbroken. The Master will assist you in becoming good for yourself, good for others, and good for Heaven's sake because, as the Bible notes (quoting an ancient philosopher named Zeno), "In Him we live and move and have our being."

I have learned that the only way to make life worth living is to throw myself with complete abandon into the tasks and challenges that come to me; to put my whole self into whatever I do, moving at a full gallop down the pathways of life.

By living in that fashion, I have discovered what an amazing place the world is, and have learned that it is filled with marvelous people. I nearly always go to bed at night with the blessed thought that I hadn't spent one minute of the day with someone I didn't want to be with, nor had I done one thing that I didn't want to do.

Five decades of studying, contemplating, writing, and speaking have brought me to the point of being wholly caught up in the amazing adventure of living with all the stops pulled out. By putting my whole self into all the activities and relationships in my life—through good times and bad, through cancer, changing economic fortunes, the deaths of people dear to me, plus through my own failures and the failures of people I have trusted—I've learned to keep undimmed the sunshine of my internal weather.

In the following pages, I'll share that learning with you.

# Introduction

The following set of 101 daily instructions provide directions, encouragement, and illustrations for taking advantage of the rich opportunities for growth and service that are available as gifts in the world around us and that have filled my own life with so much joy in living and in serving.

*How to Put Your Whole Self In* is written for the same goal as Hope Therapy, which is a psychiatric process designed to help people embrace their lives in positive ways by identifying what they actually want from life and then planning the strategies and the motivations to reach their goals. The process begins with the foundational principle that resources are available to enable people to thrive as long as we comply with the desire enunciated by Albert Einstein to accept the fact that we live in a friendly universe. My wise friend, Dr. Hugh Maiocco, echoed Einstein when he noted:

> *The Universe is an ultimately friendly place; we only need the faith to be able to see the goodness that always lies behind any façade of evil or pain, no matter how vivid they may seem.*

Coming to embrace life at this level was intentional. Anyone can live a life filled and overflowing with the good things that the Universe offers to each of us provided we possess the skills, energy, and attitudes—the willpower and "waypower"—required to make our dreams a reality.

*How to Put Your Whole Self In* will help you take advantage of the sources of power available to enable ordinary people like me to live on an extraordinary level. We find power for growth and fulfillment by working out the implications of the reality of our connections with the people around us and with Heaven above.

Two centuries ago, Herman Melville described a powerful truth:

> *We cannot live for ourselves alone. Our lives are connected by a thousand invisible threads, and along these sympathetic fibers, our actions run as causes and return to us as results.*

The following instructions will guide you in making use of the connections that Melville describes—deliberately sending actions down those "sympathetic fibers" that will return "results" that will help us be good for ourselves, good for others, and good for Heaven's sake.

Each of the "instructions" is an imperative, i.e., written as a command, and concludes with two suggested tasks for you to undertake in order to put the instruction into practice. The main content for the instruction is composed of gleanings drawn from the wisdom of others and accounts of my own experience. The instructions are arranged in three classifications:

Part I—Become a Helpful Person and a Source of Blessing
Part II—Learn Practical Truths and Bits of Wisdom
Part III—Practice Gracious Deeds and Behaviors

The pages of this book will encourage you in being a more hopeful person—one who is invigorated and inspired by challenges—possessing the ability to rebound from disappointments with no lessening of enthusiasm and hope—prepared to take advantage of every connection to be good, do good, or learn some lesson about goodness. When you read the instructions thoughtfully and incorporate them into your own beliefs, attitudes, and behaviors, they will encourage you to become more hopeful, happy, and productive.

Two final notes: Beyond the three general categories, there is no particular order in the material. The book is a compendium of wisdom, advice, and testimony—not designed to be read as though it were a novel. Savor the chapters; consider spending the next few months using this as a daily reader. Finally, you will note that the instructions contain numerous quotations. In many cases they simply help me better to express myself. The minor 19th century poet, William Ellery Channing, accurately observed:

*Quotations are true levelers.*
*They give, to all who will faithfully use them, the spiritual*
*presence of the best and greatest of the human race.*

Many of the following instructions really do offer to you, the reader, the "spiritual presence" of people far wiser than I and whose eloquence far surpasses my own. I've included these as golden jewels sewn into the fabric of my own writing.

As you read, keep in mind: the simple fact is that nothing on earth can prevent any of us from achieving our goals as long as we approach the challenges of life with appropriate attitudes. On the other hand, when weighed down by wrong attitudes, no amount of resources, status, or advantages will enable us to succeed.

# Part I

## Become a Helpful Person and a Source of Blessing

*The foundation of our lives is built upon character. The following instructions will assist you in meeting the most basic challenges involved in molding your character by encouraging the qualities, virtues, traits, and attitudes that will enable you to discover your place in the world and to perform the happy service to which Heaven has called you and equipped you to perform.*

# Day 1—Give Yourself the Gift of Living Well

*God gave us the gift of life; it is up to us to give ourselves the gift of living well. –Voltaire*

The fact is, I can't be good for anybody without being good for myself, so when the Bible tells me to love others as I love myself, it implicitly gives me a direction to love myself. The fact is that I can only become truly good for others when I have the attitudes and actions that make me good for myself.

A trusted counselor once said to me, "Don, you never criticize others, but you are always criticizing yourself." Then she added something that stopped me in my mental tracks. "You are standing in the way of your own success." The woman's gentle rebuke changed me forever because I decided on the spot that I would not ever do that again. Therefore, I now engage in the daily act of giving myself the gift of living well, as Voltaire said I should. The process for me is actually one of simply opening myself up to the heavenly sunshine of grace; experiencing in my heart the profound acceptance that The Master offers to me every day.

Such opening up to Heaven involves self-discipline. One reason why I have often not felt good about myself is the bleak truth that often there was not much to feel good about. A distinguished rabbi and philosopher Abraham J. Heschel said, "Self-respect is the fruit of discipline; the sense of dignity grows with the ability to say no to oneself." I am gradually learning the truth of Heschel's words. The solution was for me to place my life in such a position that my will could become continually bathed in the sunshine of grace, providing me with a firm basis from which to say a firm and happy "No!" to the dark side of my life. The sunlight of Heaven encourages this kind of control to grow up in my life; such Heaven-directed discipline produces a humble delight at being caught up in the wonderful, healing process.

The possibility of loving myself and not criticizing my own shortcomings is also made possible by the genuine love that I now have in my heart for other people. The Bible insists upon love in such exhortations as, "Now that you've cleaned up your lives by following the truth, love one another as if your lives depended on it" (1 Peter 1:22, The Message Translation).

One of the reasons why loving others at such a level is so important is because it then becomes relatively easy to treat myself with the same positive attitude that I display towards them. If I no longer criticize them—always forgiving them instantly for any errors in judgment or evil behaviors, even when they do them in malice to me—then it becomes possible for me to forgive myself for my own shortcomings.

I imagine that the process moves equally well in either direction. If I am blessed with genuine self-love, which is neither narcissism nor vanity, I should naturally be able to extend that love to those around me through acts of charity and forgiveness. On the other hand, as I sincerely extend love and forgiveness to others, then I'm naturally in a place to love and forgive myself.

I am avoiding the danger of becoming proud of my "success" in giving myself to others as if my life depended upon it because love and pride cancel each other; love makes us helpful to others only in the absence of any selfish pride-based motivation. I am protected from such vanity or pride as I deliberately make myself aware of the real source of, and purpose for, any such success.

The reciprocating continual movement between loving myself and loving others provides the basis for the good life that I'm living these days. So now whenever opportunity comes knocking at my door, I am unafraid to open the door and welcome with open arms whatever prospect for advancement is waiting there—glad to give myself "the gift of living well."

# Try This

1. *Identify one thing that you don't like about yourself that you want to work on.*

2. *Identify one good trait you have that helps you bless and encourage yourself. Do something with that today as a way of living well.*

# Day 2—Lead an Elevated Life

*It seems to me that people have vast potential. Most people
can do extraordinary things if they have the confidence or take
the risks. Yet most people don't. They sit in front of the TV and
treat life as if it goes on forever. —Philip Adams*

Putting my whole self into life means enabling the sense of "vast potential" that Philip Adams spoke about in this instruction's key quote. Someone said that with only 20 minutes of study a day a person could become an authority on any topic in 20 years. For example, if I could study Italian for 20 minutes each day, in two decades I could teach Italian on a University level. The greatest potential for most of us comes from practicing that kind of consistency.

My expanded life requires the quality of steadiness from me. Even more than being able to do good, I need to *be* good for the people around me—to be the worker that my partner needs, the father that my children need, the husband that my wife needs, and the man that I myself need me to be. Persistence promotes progress in each of these three areas. The demands of a moral and ethical life require that every day—from the time I get out of bed until I fall to sleep at night—that I strive with great consistency to be the man that I am supposed to be that day. By living on this elevated level over a sufficient number of days, I will lay the basis for a successful life—exhibiting the characteristics and accomplishing goals of which God himself would approve.

I am aware that being able to meet the demands of moral integrity requires of me a level of energy more powerful than mere determination. Nevertheless, I am finding persistence and integrity to be continually more effortless because every day my soul feels nourished by heavenly food; my feet again planted in a blessed place!

Many of us are inclined either to engage in a personal quest to acquire significance by our own efforts or, at the other extreme, to live in a false passivity in which we are pushed back and forth by emotions and circumstances beyond choice or control. However, I was created to be neither god nor victim. I am actually designed to be a household instrument—a vessel that can be filled with the essence of eternity, as clear water might fill a pot.

# How to Put Your Whole Self In

It took me a long time to get this straight. My life kept getting filled and choked with the clutter and garbage of random existence. I could be either somewhat up or way down according to whatever mercies or failures had accidentally slopped into my life that day. From time to time I would open the spigot of goodness a crack—in reading something uplifting, talking with a friend, or watching a sunset. However, I often remained distracted from joy by the uproar of schedule, passions, or innate folly.

My feet are regularly walking down happy and wholesome paths these days. When I realize that negative thoughts or imaginations are coming into my mind, I give them up to Heaven. The moment I realize that I have done something inappropriate to the principle of light that is in me, I seek restitution and strive to receive a fresh inflow of forgiveness that completely pulverizes any lingering effects of the darkness.

I am so grateful for the power every day to keep open a heavenly faucet and fill myself full of grace. I understand the words of James Weldon Johnson's old prayer about coming "like empty pitchers to a full fountain."

That's the way I come!

That's the kind of fountain I keep coming to.

## Try This

1.  *What have you done in the past 24 hours to make yourself good for other people?*

2.  *Determine to repeat your helpful behaviors more often. Make up your mind to do something if your answer to the first question came up blank.*

# Day 3—Be a Good Egg

*Destiny is no matter of chance. It is a matter of choice. It is not
a thing to be waited for, it is a thing to be achieved.*
*–William Jennings Bryant*

I have been on a personal mission of trying to become "a good egg"
ever since I read C.S. Lewis' stirring words:

*It may be hard for an egg to turn into a bird: it would be a
jolly sight harder for it to learn to fly while remaining an egg.
We are like eggs at present. And you cannot go on indefinitely
being just an ordinary, decent egg. We must be hatched or go
bad. –C.S. Lewis*

Unless it hatches, any good egg will become a bad egg before long—
and eventually will become a very bad egg indeed. There is no way to engage
completely in life without assuming the responsibility for shaping my destiny
rather than permitting myself to be pushed about by the winds of my passions
or by the whims of chance.

My control over life is a knife that cuts both ways. For example, an
immigrant working at a tire company who spends six years taking evening
classes at a local college and who then lands a job as office manager, ultimately
becoming the company CEO, has been overtaken by an excellent destiny that
he fashioned by his own efforts. On the other hand, a man who smokes three
to four packs of cigarettes per day for 30 years and then dies of heart disease
when he is 49 years old has been overtaken by a dreadful destiny of his own
making. Destiny can at the same time be both dreadful and excellent for the
same person. For example, the men in the two examples above might be the
same man.

In reality, destiny is a mixed bag with variables that can't be completely
controlled. For example:

- A person could lead a healthy lifestyle and die of disease
  while still in his teens.
- A person could get a Ph.D. from Stanford, fall off an
  exercise machine, striking his head, and end up mowing
  lawns for the rest of his life.
- A juvenile delinquent could rob an elderly woman of a

lottery ticket and win five million dollars.

Nevertheless, the more I regard the outcomes of my life as being within my control, the more effectively I can work on improving those outcomes. I can work at becoming a good egg.

I am grateful every day for the positive energies that keep flowing to me; thankful for a principle of grace in my life that lifts me above the vagaries of both chance and my own personality. I am living life on a higher plane than Bryant's comment allows for—a life marked by qualities like joy, love, diligence, and calmness. I am no longer young, but I say with Victor Hugo, "Winter is on my head, but eternal spring is in my heart." In spite of my calendar age, I feel new energies always coursing through me.

The healthiest people remain in pilgrimage mode—leaving behind the outworn past and moving toward the land of promise and desire. I continually have a sense that I am just getting started. The task of shaping destiny remains unfinished until life ends. The egg is always hatching, and I'll kill the life inside if I ever stop the process.

I don't know what my destiny will finally be in this world, but I am not concerned in the slightest. I can't wait to see what happens next. Somebody said, "I don't know what the future holds but I know who holds the future." That's a hopeful thing to know! Those are good hands for my destiny to be in! I can't wait to see what happens next.

# Try This

1. *Take a fearless inventory of the direction your life is going, and an honest appraisal of attitudes and behaviors on your part that are driving your life in that direction.*

2. *Determine right now to change any of the attitudes and behaviors that are driving you in directions that you don't want to go.*

# Day 4—Leave Errors Alone

*If error is corrected whenever it is recognized as such, the path of error is the path to truth. –Hans Reichenbach*

Hans Reichenbach was the founder of Berlin's School of Logical Positivism, which taught that nothing is true that cannot be demonstrated by observation and experiment—and that language involving such things as faith and belief is meaningless.

Reichenbach provides an apparently simple and effective pathway to perfection. If I can recognize and correct all the errors I commit whenever I become aware of them, then I will eventually eliminate all the errors in my life. Such an approach to improvement will prove effective, however, only if I can successfully respond to three challenges:

1. **I must be able to recognize my errors.**
   This isn't as simple a process as it might appear to be from a distance. For example, I made mistakes with my children when they were young. In retrospect, they often needed me to be both more gentle and more firm in correcting their youthful misbehaviors and rebellions. I didn't become aware of my failings to discipline them properly until the time for making effective change was long past.

2. **I must be able to correct errors when I recognize them.**
   Once again, this isn't as easy as it might appear to be since I often lack the ability to make the changes required to successfully correct my faults. Just knowing that my thought life is out of control, for example, doesn't mean that I can then take control of my thoughts; simply realizing that I keep losing my temper with my wife doesn't mean that I can control my temper.

3. **I must be able to avoid too many new errors.**
   This is another big problem since I can be as inventive as anyone else when it comes to figuring out new ways to screw things up and devising novel ways of shaming myself.

Putting myself completely into life requires me to stay away from Reichenbach's impossible "path to truth." Every day I give myself into the hands of a powerful and loving Master, and every day He gives me the power "to will and to act according to his good purpose" (Philippians 2:13)

C.S. Lewis provided a magnificent direction that we must lay before God what is in us, not what ought to be in us. Dynamic impulses for positive living are forcing out of my life the dark influences that made me so helpless to identify and fix the things that were wrong with me.

The practice of submission is no silver bullet that automatically delivers me from a struggle for goodness. Life still feels like warfare. I don't win every battle; but I am winning the war because I am engaging in the conflict with a powerful weapon. I struggle—often successfully and always with great good cheer—to turn my life over to the Master by making a whole-hearted sacrifice of intentions and plans; continually placing them into the hands of my Master. How much better is this pattern of life than attempting to engage in the onerous and ultimately futile struggle of merely trying to identify and repair errors in my life!

My engagement with life has become complete and satisfying since I quit struggling with self-improvement. My sense of fullness and fulfillment is only possible in the absence of the frustration and hypocrisy that results from any attempt to attain to a goodness that lies beyond my reach or pretending to live by a standard that I don't actually practice!!

# Try This

1. *The next time you encounter an error or failing, admit freely that once again you aren't perfect.*

2. *Hold your hands out, palms down and open (to signify that you aren't holding on to anything), and let go of the struggle. Permit The Master to fill you with His forgiveness, peace, and power.*

# Day 5—Put Away Fearfulness

*The truth that many people never understand, until it is too
late, is that the more that you try to avoid suffering, the more
you suffer, because smaller and more insignificant things begin
to torture you in proportion to your fear of being hurt.*
*—Thomas Merton*

Fear, anxiety, and worry serve to push me away from life and prevent
me from engaging in life with my whole heart. Worry never accomplishes
anything good. Mitzi Chandler, a specialist on alcoholism, codependency, and
child abuse, was exactly right when she wrote, "Worry is as useless as a handle
on a snowball."

I never spend a minute being anxious because I really do believe that
the hand of a benevolent Master is shaping the parts of my life—making
things work out for the best no matter how terrible the realities seem. My
faith in a benevolent Supreme Power delivers me from worry, since any
anxiety, in that case, would be an insult to the love and power of The Master
I am serving. Fretfulness would reveal a fundamental hypocrisy; worrying
would mean that I was trying to assume responsibility that the Master never
intended for me to have.

My goal is to possess fearlessness as a quality that the great Green Bay
Packer coach, Vince Lombardi, referred to as "mental toughness," which he
said was many things:

> *It is humility because it behooves all of us to remember that
> simplicity is the sign of greatness and meekness is the sign of
> true strength. Mental toughness is spartanism with qualities of
> sacrifice, self-denial, dedication. It is fearlessness, and it is love.*

My Grandmother Fowler once wrote a poem that began with the
words, "Worry is an awful thing; It is a form of sin…" but the poor woman
seemed to have spent the rest of her life filled with continual fretting and
worrying about the things that were happening and might be about to happen.
I never understood why she couldn't bring the shining faith that I am sure
she possessed to bear upon the difficult things that came into her life. I have
learned that worry robs me of the joy and the sense of accomplishment that

should rightfully be mine. Mary Hemingway, wife of Ernest Hemingway and an American Journalist, gave us some wise advice when she wrote:

> *Worry a little bit every day and in a lifetime you will lose a couple of years. If something is wrong, fix it if you can. But train yourself not to worry. Worry never fixes anything.*

I might have a reason for worry if I spent my energy trying to force life down a path to a particular destiny that I had picked out for myself. In that case, my attitude would be marked by dissatisfaction and anxiety, and my days full of frustration and failure. However, if I commit myself to doing the things that Heaven leads me to do, then I really am no longer responsible for the outcome. I sow the seed; God brings the harvest.

I find the solution to worry and anxiety through the healthy detachment that occurs when I am unconcerned about specific outcomes. If I wholeheartedly work with all my intelligence and strength, then I am not going to be concerned about how things turn out. Life will play itself out leaving me free to focus upon the present—not feeling any guilt about the past nor anxiety about the future, but with all my strength simply doing in the present the things that my hand finds to do. Such attitudes and actions will free me to maintain me in relationship with people whom I can encourage and who will, in turn, lift me up.

Such attitudes and actions will serve to maintain me in relationship with people whom I can encourage and who will, in turn, lift me up. The surest way to detach myself from concern for the things that will happen to me is to attach myself to an empowering purpose that will foster the habitual service for others that will enable me to put away forever and fearfulness or worry.

## Try This

1. *Make a list of 3-5 things that you've been fearful or worried about in the past.*

2. *Reflect upon the inability of your worry to affect in any way the events or people that caused you anxiety.*

# Day 6—Don't Fret About Things Like Death and Cancer

*If you can't get to 70 by an easy road, don't go.* –Mark Twain

A pastor once asked me how I was doing. I responded by saying, "Pretty good, under the circumstances."

"Well, what are you doing under the circumstances?" He asked. I thought it was a good question.

Mark Twain's admirably laconic comment about death in the key quote above reveals an important quality for anyone who desires to put their whole selves into the act of living. Fussing about death and disease serves to constrain our imaginations, to limit our spiritual powers, and to stifle our creative urges.

We are going to die; people around us are going to die. I am studiously avoiding the two mistakes we so often make at this point by not filling my mind with dark thoughts about death and disease, on one hand, and by not ignoring the reality of my own mortality and the mortality of those I love, on the other.

A number of years ago I earned the right to say that I am not overly concerned about seemingly awful realities because I had a malignancy removed in a San Francisco hospital on the same day that my mom was being cremated in a Pennsylvania mortuary.

Even then, at no point did I find myself "under the circumstances." Overall, it really wasn't too bad a day. My mind was at ease and my spirit peacefully resigned to the shocks that God had brought me to.

Of course, cancer is no trifling matter. The initial diagnosis came as a shock but I ceased fretting once the processes of resignation kicked in. I was relieved. Following the surgery I was relieved when the surgeon came back with a report that no cancer cells had showed up in my lymph glands. However, what if they had? How could I have complained even if it had turned out I were to die of cancer?

My brother-in-law, Rodney, one of the most likeable, fun-loving people I ever knew, succumbed to sarcoma when he was only 13 years old. Any of us in the family would have gladly given our lives to spare his. Better people than I am have died of far worse things than cancer. Anne Frank died in a concentration camp. The body of the renowned scientist, Stephen Hawking, has been dying by inches for more than four decades. Jesus died on the cross.

I think Heaven never responds to the question, "Why me?" about any circumstance that could arise in my life because the real answer, bound up in the rejoinder question, "Why not me?" is too obvious to bother with. The process of coming to heart-filled resignation is eased by my daily deliberate acceptance of the deeper reality underlying all outward circumstances, no matter how grim—that my life and my times are held in Hands that will not drop me, no matter what comes my way. There's a purpose in every passing circumstance, whether I can discern the purpose, or not. "Underneath are the everlasting arms." They really are!

Coping with my mom's passing was another demonstration of the power of grace over circumstance. I admit that death is an awful thing. It is the great Enemy! The Destroyer! I hate it! Nevertheless, something marvelous surrounds the death of any person like my mom that serves to overwhelm the forces of desolation and bleakness.

I told people who asked about my reaction to my mom's passing, "I have done a lot of bawling, but I haven't been sad for a moment." Many of my listeners nodded their heads and smiled. They knew exactly what I was saying; there was nothing remarkable about my attitude.

That Friday when I had surgery and my mom was buried was a good day. I was living above the circumstances of cancer and death.

# Try This

1. *Reflect on the experiences of people like Anne Frank, Stephen Hawking, and Jesus who put their whole selves into the acts of living in spite of the grim things they experienced.*

2. *Write the sentence, "I am not going to live under my circumstances." Post it on your mirror, refrigerator, or any place where you will see it regularly.*

# Day 7—Remain Busy with Happy Activities

*Blessed is the person who is too busy to worry in the daytime
and too sleepy to worry at night. –Anonymous*

The word "busy" has negative connotations if my busyness is filled with activities that keep me from maintaining close relationships with Heaven and with the people around me. However, if my life is filled with activities of service for The Master and for others—and if I am creatively engaging with the world—then I am able to live above the frets, worries, and concerns that otherwise would be pulling me down.

I am in the cheerful place of being "too busy to worry in the daytime and too sleepy to worry at night." The pace of my life has gone from merely hectic to absolutely furious because I am developing my career as an author and a motivational speaker while writing and ghostwriting most of the articles in our monthly magazine plus ghostwriting as many as four books at a time. I am working seven days every week, and get more work done on vacation than when I am in the office because there are fewer distractions.

People might be tempted to feel sorry for me working like this—or, more likely, be tempted to consider me crazy—but the fact is every night I go to bed thankful for the experiences of the day because almost always I hadn't done a single thing I didn't want to do nor had I spent a minute with someone whom I wished would go away.

I am an especially blessed person at this point because almost none of the activities that I do are driven by external schedules:

- My work activities are 100% self-directed. I am responsible for designing, scheduling, and implementing the tasks I undertake.
- I am in the middle of reading several wonderful books. I don't have time to read as much as I wish.
- I never have enough time for dear friends. I would like to spend hours or days with them—a lifetime, in many cases.
- I never have time to play computer games as much as I would like.
- My wife, Rae, and I like to watch several TV shows—and a lot more that we would watch if we had time.
- I try to spend a half-hour a day on my Wii Fit exercise program, and always wish that I could spend more time on that marvelous device.

# How to Put Your Whole Self In

In the words of John Denver,

> *There's a spirit that guides me;*
> *A light that shine's for me;*
> *My life's worth the living;*
> *I don't need to see the end."*

Remaining busily involved in activities that engage my attention and my passion might be one of the ways to help ensure my success in life. At least that was Thoreau's opinion, because he wrote. "Success usually comes to those who are too busy to be looking for it."

Lee Iacocca, the former CEO of Chrysler, found another purpose in keeping busy besides assisting us towards success. He considered energetic and enthusiastic activities to provide effective antidotes to conditions that might cause us to become discouraged or depressed. "In times of great stress or adversity," he wrote, "it's always best to keep busy, to plow your anger and your energy into something positive."

I continually feel like I am receiving the blessing promised by God in the Bible, "Open your mouth wide and I will fill it" (Psalm 81:10). I open myself fully to the grace of Heaven and, in return, Heaven fills my life with good things. By the time I finally tear myself away from joy-filled activities and go to bed, sleep usually comes like a blessed benediction—nothing to regret; nothing to fear.... Maybe this is the best thing of all.

# Try This

1. *Make two columns—on the left list the things you most enjoy; on the right the things you least enjoy.*

2. *Deliberately plan to fill your life more with the things on the left column and to decide how to minimize the items on the right—or perhaps create a plan for enjoying those things that you may have been missing.*

# Day 8—Kick Bad Habits

*Habit is habit and not to be flung out of the window by*
*any man, but coaxed downstairs a step at a time.*
*–Mark Twain*

The quality of my inner and outer life is determined to a considerable extent, by forces of good and evil that I strengthen or starve by my patterns of thinking, reacting, and meditating.

I came to a moment of clarity years ago, when my Aunt Iris posed a question for me: "We have two dogs fighting inside of us, a black dog and a white dog, Donnie. Which dog wins the fight?" The answer turned out to be "The one you feed."

Most of us fail to engage completely in life because of bad habits and learned behaviors that inhibit such full engagement. Therefore, one of my most important personal tasks is the breaking of habits that waste my time, damage my relationship with the people around me, limit my ability to explore the possibilities of life, and harm my health. I have had habits that worked against my effectiveness as a human being. My wife can attest that I am a naturally slothful, undisciplined kind of individual.

Getting rid of destructive habits while at the same time forming positive ones is a difficult task, of course. My big problem is that developing any good habit requires a great deal of energy and continual reinforcement, whereas bad habits develop with little or no effort on my part. I am so grateful that a principle of grace has invaded my life and has invested me with a power sufficient to make fundamental changes in the ways I habitually live—in the thoughts I routinely think and in the things I consistently do. As a result, my life is regularly becoming a happier place to live, constantly more filled with grace.

Developing good habits isn't an overnight process, as Mark Twain pointed out in the instruction's key quote. I have to coax my habits "downstairs, a step at a time" just as he did. The Roman philosopher, Seneca, wrote:

# How to Put Your Whole Self In

*It is easier to exclude harmful passions than to rule them,*
*and to deny them admittance than to control them after*
*they have been admitted.*

I can agree with Seneca based on my own personal experience, which is why my New Year's Resolutions always fail; I lack sufficient energy to change the course of my life in the fundamental ways that making good habits demands. I am thankful, however, that by the influences and promptings of Heaven I began developing good habits to overcome the negative ones.

I am done with New Year's Resolutions. Once a year provides far too infrequent a cadence for setting rhythms and resonances that could change the habitual ways in which I think and behave. I try to reset each day—meditating on the thoughts that should occupy my mind, and striving to become again the man that Heaven, other people, and my family needs me to be.

I daily take the internal and external steps that will enable me actually to lift my spirit to Heaven, to stand erect before Him, and to welcome proudly and humbly the light that is becoming part of my life. I am coaxing my bad habits "downstairs a step at a time," as Mark Twain said I should. I am regularly feeding the white dog with good stuff these days. I have learned where the black dog food is and I am starving that mutt.

# Try This

1. *Write down on a piece of paper one bad habit you want to get rid of and one good one you wish to cultivate.*

2. *Below each, note one action you are going to take for each of these to "coax" them downstairs.*

# Day 9—Find People Beautiful

*There is no excellent beauty that hath not some strangeness in the proportion.* –Francis Bacon

Finding other people to be beautiful plays an important role in my remaining engaged with other people.

When I first read Bacon's words, they stopped me in my tracks because I instantly recognized how profoundly true they are. I am often strongly moved by the beauty and grace of things that seem superficially flawed and imperfect. The poem, "I am a little church," by ee cummings, for example, seems to me to be one of the most compelling literary works I ever read, but imagine a traditional copy editor receiving the following:

*winter by spring, I lift my diminutive spire to
merciful Him Whose only now is forever:
standing erect in the deathless truth of His presence
—welcoming humbly His light and proudly His darkness*

From a formal point of view, the poem is a grammatical mess. Punctuation is missing or mistaken. Words are in the incorrect order. Adjectives don't really fit with words they modify. The only capitalized words are capitalized incorrectly. Everything about it is "wrong." From a superficial point of view, the thing is obviously in serious need of a complete rewrite. Nevertheless, in putting together an anthology of American poetry no editor would touch one character of the poem. It would hardly be correct to say that Cummings poem works in spite of all the "errors." In some strange way (at least for those of us who "get" Cummings) the poem works precisely because of the unconventional elements—the "strangeness in the proportion," to use Bacon's words.

I believe in the principle of finding beauty in imperfection when it comes to people. I have always pushed away as too dismissive Shakespeare's famous comment that "Beauty is in the eye of the beholder." Common beauty extends much farther than mere internalization of attitudes. My eye truly recognizes rather than merely creates the beauty I see in people around me.

When I learn to put my whole self into relationships with people such things as crooked teeth, skin blemishes, veins, and wrinkles all become part of the beauty of the people whom I have come to love. The attractiveness of a beloved person somehow becomes enhanced by the lack of porcelain-perfect complexions or god-like bodies. Some people I dearly love have lost 30 pounds who I thought looked fine before they started. People I cherish have paid thousands of dollars for teeth alignments when I thought they were beautiful before the operation.

I also see in many people the inward beauty that the Bible talks about: a beauty from the "inner self, the unfading beauty of a gentle and quiet spirit" (1 Peter 3:4) The Bible then adds about this kind of beauty, that it "is of great worth in God's sight." Right! And in my sight too!

Perhaps the quality of my feelings, prompted as they are by the grace of Heaven, is accurately reflected in the words of a chorus we used to sing:

*I can see in you the glory of my King*
*And I love you with the love of the Lord.*

I am so thankful that Heaven puts in my heart the capacity for seeing beauty in others and for acknowledging that the outward appearance of an inwardly beautiful person is only enhanced by whatever "strangeness" there might be "in the proportion." Hollywood creates a beautiful illusion; The Master creates a beautiful essence that I can see and touch, and that calls my mind to joy, delight, and sometimes to worship.

# Try This

1. *Determine today to search for the inner beauty of somebody who is close to you. Thank them for sharing that part of their inner self with you.*

2. *Observe how the small act changed your attitude. Do this habitually and it will change your life.*

# Day 10—Rejoice in Working

*You never achieve real success unless you like what you are doing. –Dale Carnegie*

A malaise seemingly abroad in our culture causes many people to regard life as bleak and colorless in spite of the fact that most of us work at jobs that are incredible by the standards of a third of the world's population, who are typically doing things like planting rice, and scavenging for food and firewood. I seem to have bypassed the problem of viewing my job in a bad light, since I really love what I do—which makes me at least partially successful when judged by Dale Carnegie's criteria in his key quote for this instruction. By any normal standard of judging, however, I lived most of my life as a very mitigated success indeed with neither fame nor fortune. I recently spent a whole decade without a stable source of income.

I am frankly unconcerned about success as judged by the common standards of status and wealth, because while I drive my life in upward directions by my attitudes and decisions, the fact is that I am not ultimately responsible either for my successes or failures, so I am content to leave my successes as well as my failures in the hands of my Master. In fact, I am not wise enough to tell what is ultimately good or bad in the events of life so that I am even leaving Him to judge which actions and outcomes belong in which category. Nevertheless, I am successful by the one criterion that Dale Carnegie mentions in the key quote for this instruction. I really like what I am doing. I find my writing and speaking tasks to be more satisfying than going to Disneyland. I love the life I am living!

Satisfaction in a person's work depends 90 percent upon attitude and only 10 percent upon the nature of the job. Job satisfaction comes especially from an aim at excellence, following the advice Lincoln gave: "Whatever you are, be a good one."

I agree with Carnegie that success comes from doing work you enjoy doing. People who don't like their job should seek out a profession that they do like. With the right attitude, however, I can sometimes find a third alternative: I can nearly always find something to like in almost any situation.

# How to Put Your Whole Self In

Years ago, to help put myself through school, I spent two summers operating a boxing machine in a meat packing company. I am not a naturally quick person and it took me a while to learn how to efficiently operate that device. However, I eventually became the best box machine operator the company had ever seen, I think. Even though it was a repetitive boring job, I found ways to make it challenging and satisfying. Time went fast. One way I found to overcome the tedium of the job was to keep my mind filled with positive thoughts and ideassinging songs, quoting proverbs and poems I had memorized, saying prayers, and writing poetry in my mind.

I don't run a boxing machine anymore, of course. I work at a profession that many people would consider to be rewarding. But I am doing my job in the same way that I performed my tasks as a professional boxing machine operator; I am trying to be the best I can be at what I do—continually looking for ways to be good and to do good. I expect my job to be happy and satisfying.

So of course, I am achieving success by Dale Carnegie's definition! With such an attitude, how could I miss?

# Try This

1. *Find somebody today and tell him/her the thing you like most about your job/profession/life.*

2. *Change your job, if you must. Until then, seek out the areas that bring you fulfillment and happiness. Continually focus on those.*

# Day 11—Cultivate Hopeful Humility

*I am defeated and know it if I meet any human being from*
*whom I find myself unable to learn anything.*
*—George Herbert Palmer*

An essential requirement for putting my whole self into relationships is the ability to relate to anybody irrespective of their position in society, level of education, or any other status indicator. Such ability requires a hopefully humble attitude. Galileo Galilei—a physicist, mathematician, astronomer, and philosopher, who was called the Father of Modern Science—revealed true greatness of spirit when he said, "I have never met a man so ignorant that I couldn't learn something from him." I am still in the process of developing the ability to learn from anybody.

One winter evening on a street corner in San Francisco's Theater District, I noticed a homeless person sitting in the entrance of a nearby alleyway. He was holding a crude sign with the words, "AIDS victim. Help if you can." By itself, a beggar with a sign was not a remarkable occurrence on the streets of San Francisco, but at the bottom of the sign a large handwritten note said, "If all you can afford to give me is a smile, I'll return it to you." That note made me look at the person himself for the first time. He was seriously wasted by his disease and stared back at me from shrunken eye sockets. Nevertheless, in response to that note, I smiled at him. The man's face was instantly transformed by the most beaming and beatific smile I ever saw in my life. The man's smile was like a window opening into a green and sunlit place. When I hurried over to place a gift into his coffee can, he responded with what seemed to be genuine delight at the effectiveness of his little ploy.

I learned a lesson about the power of connections that day from the wretched beggar. In some way, the experience changed my attitude towards suffering in general and towards homeless people in particular. I imagine that such lessons can only be learned by people who have some degree of genuine humility.

C.S. Lewis maintained that humility is an often-misunderstood virtue. According to Lewis, the essence of true humility is for me to regard the virtues and talents of the people around me with as much delight as I regard my own. The sign of a humble heart, Lewis claimed, is when I imagine that

## How to Put Your Whole Self In

I am surrounded by wonderfully gifted and admirable people. However, the sun of my life reaches its zenith when I find delight in serving other people whether or not they seem deserving of my attention—to serve them even if I derive no profit from doing so. A moving exhortation about servanthood is ascribed to Mother Teresa:

*People are illogical, unreasonable, and self-centered.*
   *Love them anyway.*
*The good you do today will be forgotten tomorrow.*
   *Do good anyway.*
*Honesty and frankness make you vulnerable.*
   *Be honest and frank anyway.*
*What you spend years building may be destroyed overnight.*
   *Build anyway.*
*People really need help, but may attack you if you do help them.*
   *Help them anyway.*
*Give the world the best you have and you'll get kicked in the teeth.*
   *Give the world the best you have anyway.*
*You see, in the final analysis, it is between you and God.*
*It was never between you and them anyway.*

A principle of grace affecting me these days is both produced by and produces a proper attention of my mind and intention of my heart towards others. I am humbly delighted to be in service of others. I am especially grateful to be surrounded by remarkable people. I often marvel that The Master has filled my life full of these people from whom I receive innumerable gifts. Even a disease-wracked beggar can, on occasion, give me a small gift of such astonishing grace that its memory remains with me forever.

# Try This

1.   *Reflect on a time when you were able to learn from someone else a lesson about living or even about joy.*

2.   *Spend some time looking into the lives of other people to find some lesson that will help you engage more fully in life.*

## Day 12—Remain Connected to the Source

*If you know that all is well, you know all you need to know.*
*And if you know life is supposed to be fun, you know more*
*than almost anybody else knows. And if you know that the*
*way you feel is your indicator of how connected you are to the*
*Source, then you know that which only a handful of Deliberate*
*Creators, respective to the total population, really know.*
*—Esther Hicks*

Before I discovered that wellness and fun were connected with a Source that made them possible, I was unable to realize the shining purposes that the Source—Destiny, Angels, God, or however it manifest itself—was putting in my way.

Jesus illustrated the connection that Esther Hicks spoke about in the key quote by comparing it to the essential relationship that branches maintain with a grapevine in order to remain healthy and productive. Maintaining that connection is the only struggle that I have these days. Once the link is in place, qualities like peace, joyfulness, love, and kindness come as effortlessly as fruit comes to a healthy branch and keep me orderly, happy, and productive.

Even though I am not a committed follower of Esther Hicks' philosophy, as she presented it in *The Secret*, the key quote above correctly identifies the connection between a sense of wellness and fun to a Source. I probably would define the Source differently than Hicks' definition, but I agree with the connection that she finds.

People avoid fully engaging with the world or with the lives of the people around them because of fear for what might result from such engagement. Such people miss the fact that life lived on that level is, in fact, fun. "God's in His Heaven; All's right with the world" is Robert Browning's famous line spoken in defiance of despair. Nothing could seem more doubtful to a skeptic than the accuracy of Browning's assertion. The line points to one of the main paradoxes that life uncovers when we engage with it completely.

Life was simple and contained no hidden complexities as long as I chose to remain at a superficial level and avoid any deeper engagement than to simply react to the events and other stimuli of each day as I encountered them. However, as I began to reflect upon the meaning of life and to engage in life at a more complete level, I began to encounter complications.

The deeper I engage in life the more conscious I become of the truth that was pointed out by the great mathematician and philosopher, Blaise Pascal, that "Contradiction is not a sign of falsity, nor the lack of contradiction a sign of truth." On that level I really can believe that "all is well." Hick's affirmation is all that I need to believe. If all is well, than why should we have fun?

Believing that "all's well," is a requirement for the full engagement of life that I am experiencing. If I really believe that, then no matter how difficult a circumstance may be, some good can always be found to redeem the evil. No matter how wicked a person may seem, some good can always be found that could draw the person to the light. As long as I really believe that from my heart, I always am able to find the good.

As far as I can remember, every one of the people I encountered while writing articles for my lifestyle magazine and the writers I have ghostwritten books for have been conscious of a connection with a Benevolent Power in the Universe about them—and all of them consider the Power to be personal. Most think of the power as God—in a few cases as an angelic messenger.

I have discovered that the way they described the Source of positive energy mattered little; the fact that they were connected to it was everything.

# Try This

1. *Take some time right now to reflect upon the Source of the things that come into your life.*

2. *Take a moment to embrace the reality that the Universe has a smiling face, even though it may sometimes be hidden behind seemingly dark circumstances.*

# Day 13—Follow the Path of Integrity

*Never esteem anything as of advantage to thee that shall make*
*thee break thy word or lose thy self-respect.—Marcus Aurelius*

Complete integrity—"the quality of possessing and steadfastly adhering to high moral principles or professional standards"—is required before I can sincerely embrace the world or the people around me. Integrity is the basis of Marcus Aurelius' standard recorded in this instruction's key quote.

Aurelius was a great philosopher but during the final 19 years of his life, when he was the Roman Emperor, he certainly failed to live up to his own declared standard. He raised a perfectly monstrous son, Commodus (as everyone knows who saw the movie *Gladiator*). In addition, Aurelius was a terrible persecutor of the church. Did the man who raised Commodus and who martyred Christians retain his "self-respect"?

The words in Aurelius' quote resonate with Polonius' famous advice to Laertes:

*This above all: to thine own self be true*
*And it must follow, as the night the day*
*Thou canst not then be false to any man.*

Polonius never took his own advice. He was a blackguard and a rascal; a spineless tattletale, whom Hamlet contemptuously dismissed with the words, "...that great baby you see there is not yet out of his swaddling-clouts."

I am sure that Aurelius and Polonius would willingly have become better people if they could have managed it, but doing so lay beyond their reach. In that respect, they were just like I was for most of my life. I couldn't live up to the standards of my own philosophies and aspirations any better than they lived up to theirs. Since discovering, however, that the powers of Heaven are available to help me live justly and joyfully in this world, I have become a person of integrity—one without guile.

The growing quality of integrity provides an escape from any sense that life is a meaningless existence. The movie *Life Stinks*, has an improbable plot concerning two street people, named Goddard and Molly. When Goddard falls into an apparently fatal coma in the hospital, Molly comes to him and, bending over him, tells him that life is wretched but with occasional moments of beauty. "That's what life is. Just a bunch of moments," she says. "Most of them are lousy, but once in a while you get a good one."

A number of people live life at that level—enduring their awful jobs and their wretched lives for the sake of the few moments of beauty that come along. The possibility is always held out to me, however, when I engage in life with complete honesty and integrity, of living each day with such a quivering sense of destiny that my eyes become opened to the reality of the grace in which I can live and move—and then to see the golden moments as they come.

Integrity must surely be one of the basic qualities of a well-lived life. "Better to be poor than a liar." the Bible says (Proverbs 19:22). What is required is that each day—each moment, insofar as I can do so—without deceit or deception I give myself into the hands of my Master. He takes my life from me; then He gives it back in a renewed version.

I am so grateful for the freedom that is mine in this life that I am now living; thankful indeed for the power to fight against the dark side of my character. By God's help, I do not break my word; with Heaven's help I am true to myself, to others, and to Him above all.

# Try This

1. *Make a fearless assessment of your life and resolve to amend your behavior in any area in which you are not behaving in an honest and forthright manner.*

2. *Resolve to not look for or to expect others to live up to the standard of integrity that you should insist upon from yourself.*

# Day 14—Stand Against Gossip

*Be gentle to all, and stern with yourself.*
*—Saint Teresa of Avila*

In this instruction's key quote, Saint Teresa reverses attitudes that are all too common and that would formerly get me into trouble. My natural instinct was to be stern with others and gentle on myself—forgiving things that I would do myself for which I would criticize and judge others when they would do it. My attitude was the worse kind of hypocrisy because it prevented me from doing anything to correct my own faults while cutting others off from the love and affection that they deserved from me. Such a hypocritical spirit is an old problem because the Bible says:

> *You, therefore, have no excuse, you who pass judgment on someone else, for at whatever point you judge the other, you are condemning yourself, because you who pass judgment do the same things (Romans 2:1).*

Or, in the clear rewording of the Message Translation: "Judgmental criticism of others is a well-known way of escaping detection in your own crimes and misdemeanors." Only by following the admonition of Saint Teresa and the Bible can I really reach out to others because we are good for each other to the extent we embrace one another without paying attention to whatever faults or shortcomings we might notice.

I'm dismissive concerning gossip even about myself. I easily forgive another person for gossiping about me because what good can ever be gained by trying to get even with the person—or even trying to correct the gossip? When someone says something bad about me, even when it is not true, I just let it go—consoling myself with the sure knowledge that the truth will eventually drive away the falsehood. While I forgive gossipers for their slander, whether or not they ever apologize for their actions, I maintain an absolute standard against participating in gossip myself—not listening to it or, much less, spreading it. If I am at least willing to put myself wholeheartedly into a relationship then what good could possibly be served by my spreading negative information about the person whether or not it is true?

# How to Put Your Whole Self In

When rightly understood, the other part of Saint Teresa's standard—of being "stern" with myself—is also essential to pursuing the best possible relationship with others. While it is important for me to accept myself with all my faults, just as I accept others, it is vitally important for me not to become satisfied or complacent about myself and my actions. As soon as I realize that I myself have offended someone, I must go to the person and make whatever apologies or amends I can—seeking their forgiveness without saying one word in my own defense. I always appreciated Father Fulton J. Sheen's observation:

> *The good are not always good in all things, and the wicked are not always wicked in all things. As it has been said, 'There is so much good in the worst of us and so much bad in the best of us,' that it ill behooves any of us to talk about the rest of us.*

There is nobody in my life that I can't learn something from; nobody who doesn't have some qualities that I can admire; nobody who hasn't done some things that I can respect and even praise him/her for. As a result, there is nobody about whom I am willing to repeat anything I hear that the person wouldn't want shared in public. I put my whole self into my relationships with others only by pulling myself out of negative conversations about anybody.

# Try This

1. *The next time you hear somebody spreading some rumor about another person, share with the person some failing or fault of your own that will cast the person gossiped about in a more forgiving light.*

2. *Never harshly rebuke or castigate gossipers, since that would diminish the closeness of your relationship with them. If they don't learn from your example, just let it go. You aren't responsible for their choices.*

# Day 15—Put into Practice Einstein's Other Formula

*A + B + C = Success if*
*A = Hard Work*
*B = Hard Play*
*C = Keeping your mouth shut.*

The third element—the "C" in Einstein's formula—elevates the expression from being an aphorism to a profound truth. I build barriers between others and myself when I do not control my tongue! An old proverb says, "He who guards his mouth and his tongue keeps himself from calamity."

I am glad to work hard, as Einstein said I should. I am thankful that I also have fun at play. However, I am most grateful that I sometimes find the grace to hold my tongue.

Thomas Edison once reportedly offered some wry advice, "You will have many opportunities in life to keep your mouth shut: You should take advantage of every one of them." Mark Twain pressed his caustic wit into the service of restraining our mouths when he wrote, "Noise proves nothing." Then he added, "Often a hen who has merely laid an egg cackles as if she had laid an asteroid."

I have seldom regretted a failure to speak up, though I have often later regretted things that I have said. One of the resources that assists me in keeping my words fewer and sweeter is the knowledge earned by personal experiences of how damaging my tongue can be. "Sticks and stones may break my bones but words can never hurt me," is a lie we used to chant when I was a child. In fact, words hurt far worse than any sticks and stones. With their tongues people opened wounds in my soul decades ago that I still carry with me. Moreover, I, in turn, have harmed others with my words—damaging them far beyond the ability of any powers I possess to heal the harm that I inflicted. The Bible says:

> *The tongue ... is a fire, a world of evil among the parts of the body. It corrupts the whole person, sets the whole course of his life on fire, and is itself set on fire by hell (James 3:6).*

# How to Put Your Whole Self In

Silence is golden and becomes so in more ways than by simply refraining from saying bad things; I am also learning not always to attempt to say something good, profound, or humorous. Nothing requires me to strive to make an impression by my speech; I don't always have to try to fix something with my words.

I am learning the virtue of silence. We comfort each other in times of distress by our hugs and by our tears—not by our words nor by any attempted explanations about the situation. My daughter's little doggie, Roxanne, is one of the most loving and loveable creatures on the planet. She senses when a person is feeling depressed and provides solace in her little doggy fashion. Of course, Roxie communicates affection and consolation without uttering a single word. Being granted the ability to speak would probably diminish the effectiveness of her communication.

I am thankful that I am doing a little better with my mouth these days. I often let opportunities to criticize pass by. I keep silent sometimes when I am tempted to "speak my mind." I try to use only soothing words to express ideas that will preserve harmony and bring peace. During those times of restraint I really do feel that I have managed to do something good in this world. In addition, sometimes, when I am at my best, circumstances are able to make a song of my silence. Einstein was right. It's a success to learn to keep my mouth shut. Moreover, it feels good!

# Try This

1.  *For the next day deliberately look for opportunities to remain silent during circumstances that would normally have prompted you to some angry or critical comment.*

2.  *Learn from some beloved family pet how to communicate without using words and sentences.*

# Day 16—Look for the Good; Accentuate the Positive

*The open-minded see the truth in different things: the narrow-minded see only the differences. —Anonymous*

Ever since I have quit looking for problems, failures, and things to criticize in other people's lives and even in my own, I've been able to put my whole-hearted engagement into the Universe and the people around me. My positive attitude towards life and towards others is the product that comes from deliberate choices that I make every day. The Vietnamese monk, teacher, author, poet, and peace activist, Thich Nhat Hanh, maintained an important truth:

*Though we all have the fear and the seeds of anger within us, we must learn not to water those seeds and instead nourish our positive qualities—those of compassion, understanding, and loving kindness.*

I am learning to have a positive response to difficult situations, looking for lessons from whatever happens to me, not leaving room in my heart for feelings of disappointment and discouragement. Whenever Depression knocks on the door of my heart, I send Hopefulness to answer the door.

I really am in charge of my own emotions, whether peaceful or stormy. If someone cuts me off in traffic, it is inaccurate to say that the person *made* me angry. Nobody can *make* me angry. The only thing that happens is that the person's action simply brings out the anger that I had in my spirit. Jesus wouldn't have been angered in that situation, for example. Or Gandhi. Or Mother Teresa. They would have remained serene because each of them had no reservoir of anger that could have spilled over in an angry response.

I am increasingly more sorrowful when I encounter mean-spirited and morose people. The worst cases are grumpy elderly people. It is disappointing that people could live five decades (or nine decades) and somehow never learn the lesson that they were in charge of their emotions. It is a terrible failure! Only spiritually weak people could burden themselves for a lifetime beneath a weight of negative emotions.

Grumpy people imagine that circumstances such as the loss of health or betrayal by some trusted person created their disagreeable attitude towards life; they remain stoutly resistant to the cheerful condition of people who suffered much more than they. Victor Frankl, for example, faced the worst that life could offer for three years in German concentration camps during which his wife and parents were murdered, and where he witnessed the death of many people. Following the experience, Frankl announced a shining principle:

> We who lived in concentration camps can remember the men who walked through the huts comforting others, giving away their last piece of bread. They may have been few in number, but they offer sufficient proof that everything can be taken from a man or a woman but one thing: the last of human freedoms, to choose one's attitude in any given set of circumstances, to choose one's own way.

The poet Maya Angelou—whose life of sexual childhood abuse, guilt, and five years as a mute read like something out of a Stephen King novel—came to the point where she could write, "If you don't like something, change it. If you can't change it, change your attitude. Don't complain."

We need to remain positive in the face of the most discouraging circumstance because, as Helen Keller told us, "No pessimist ever discovered the secret of the stars, or sailed to an uncharted land, or opened a new doorway for the human spirit." Each day is a gift from the Master, and while life may not always seem fair, I will never allow the pains, hurdles, and handicaps of the moment to poison my attitude and plans for myself.

# Try This

1. *The next time some discouraging circumstance comes along, take control of your negative feelings. Don't discount them but work through them.*

2. *When a person offends you, respond positively. Don't permit anyone to steal your sense of joy.*

# Day 17—Listen Up!

*When you are listening to somebody, completely, attentively,*
*then you are listening not only to the words, but also to the*
*feeling of what is being conveyed, to the whole of it, not part of*
*it. –Jiddu Krishnamurti*

One of the most effective ways of involving myself completely in the lives of other people is by listening carefully to them whenever they are speaking to me. The English author and journalist, Rebecca West, offered a tongue-in-cheek but piercing standard for interpersonal communication when she wrote, "There was a definite process by which one made people into friends." Then she defined the "definite process" in a single phrase: "It involved talking to them and listening to them for hours at a time."

One of my friends is blind in one eye. Because he was unable to use peripheral vision, he was forced to look directly at anyone speaking to him. One day someone commented to him on what a good listener he was. My friend realized that he gave that impression because his impairment forced him to continually look directly at anybody who was speaking to him. I imagine that the act of looking at the person really did serve to improve my friend's listening skills.

Effective listening seems to be in decline in our society, which is a shame because the art of listening opens doorways to many wonderful things in this world. For example, someone said that leadership involves "the ability to see what no one else sees, to listen when others talk and the ability to be optimistic when others are pessimistic."

Showing people that I care about them can involve nothing more than merely listening to them when they speak. Dr. Joyce Brothers claims that such listening, rather than imitation, is the sincerest form of flattery. Perhaps qualities such as affection, respect, and admiration are basic building blocks for good communication since they encourage what must be the best attitude for a careful listener: "I am listening carefully to everything you say because I don't want to miss anything."

Some people are boring because they subconsciously use speech as a way of remaining disengaged from the people around them. The most effective method for not communicating with another person, perhaps, is to just create a flow of words that will deny the listener an opportunity to speak, drowning the possibility of conversation beneath a flood of monologue.

Three centuries ago, an Italian jurist, named Gian Vincenzo Gravina, created one of the world's most elegant definitions when he said that, "A bore is a man who deprives you of solitude without providing you with company." However, C.S. Lewis provided an important caveat: "The man who lets himself be bored is even more contemptible than the bore." The most obvious interpretation of Lewis' comment is the view that any intelligent person should find a way to disengage from a boring conversation, but I think that Lewis wrote that because he knew that there are ways of engaging with even a boring person that might draw the person into animated conversation. Perhaps finding something about the person to admire: "I wanted to tell you how much I admired that comment you made last week." Or perhaps a comment expressing affection: "I am glad that we're able to be together on the committee."

The point is, that boring people deserve our love. Everyone at heart has a longing expressed by the appeal someone made, "You might not hear my words, but just look into my eyes and listen with your heart." Even those who bore us are sending us messages beneath their chatter to which we should listen.

# Try This

1. *For the next 24 hours concentrate on looking directly with both eyes at everyone who is speaking to you. Listen to what they say. Listen to what they aren't saying out loud.*

2. *During this time try to direct conversations into topics that will serve to promote the quality of your relationship to others. Speak words that are supportive, positive, and loving.*

# Day 18—Find Your Purpose

*The purpose of life is not to be happy. It is to be useful, to be honorable, to be compassionate, to have it make some difference that you have lived and lived well. —Ralph Waldo Emerson*

My life moved into its current happy and productive state as I began to realize the purpose for which I was put on this earth—to lift others by my writing and by my motivational speaking. My path led through a number of byways before I finally came to realize the work that the Master had planned for me to do, but I will not call them detours. The fact is that I wouldn't be the person I am—nor would I have the abilities that I possess, nor the wisdom that I have come to—if my life had been different at any point. The roads I have taken are more important than any goals because the journey wasn't leading towards life but was life itself.

The discovery of my reason for living has brought me to a happy place indeed. Helen Keller accurately noted that, "Many persons have a wrong idea of what constitutes true happiness. It is not attained through self-gratification but through fidelity to a worthy purpose." I am determined to make a profit through all my writing and speaking activities, but the "bottom line" is not my ultimate goal. The hand of the Master has brought me to this place in order that I might make a positive impact upon the world.

My greatest satisfaction comes from being "useful," to use Emerson's word from this instruction's key quote. I understand completely the Olympian champion Eric Liddell's comment, "I believe God made me for a purpose, but he also made me fast. And when I run I feel His pleasure." My particular purpose in living is intensely personal in the same way—a conviction that I have come to following years of experience, learning, and growth. I share the conviction Oprah spoke about when she said:

> *I have come to believe that each of us has a personal calling that's as unique as a fingerprint—and that the best way to succeed is to discover what you love and then find a way to offer it to others in the form of service, working hard, and also allowing the energy of the universe to lead you.*

## How to Put Your Whole Self In

Then Oprah added an essential summary, "The reward of a thing well done is to have done it." Oprah's comment points to service as an essential element of every genuine purpose. Everybody on earth who has learned how to genuinely put their whole selves into life is sharing the ultimate goal of being able to say with sincerity, "The world is a better place because I am in it." I'm trying to live in such a way that when I die good people will mourn by my casket.

Carl Jung, the founder of analytical psychology, declared, "As far as we can discern, the sole purpose of existence is to kindle a light in the darkness of being." No purpose for my life could ever bring me into full engagement with life and into healthy relationships with the people around me that doesn't embody in some way that fundamental purpose of brightening the world about me. Marion Wright Edelman, founder of the Children's Defense Fund, caught the heart of the matter when she wrote, "Service is the rent we pay for being. It is the very purpose of life, and not something you do in your spare time."

Only by being good for others and for Heaven's sake can I really be good for myself and discover real joy. The English poet and hymn-writer William Cowper wrote the words, "The only true happiness comes from squandering ourselves for a purpose."

## Try This

1.  *Fill in the blank to the question: "My purpose and calling in life is to _____."*

2.  *Consider your answer carefully. Make certain about this. Seek for guidance if you are unsure or if the purpose seems too limited in the service it offers to others and to Heaven.*

# Day 19—Dance to the Rhythms

*(A devil speaking) If we neglect our duty, men will not only be contented but transported by the mixed novelty and familiarity of snowdrops this January, sunrises this morning, plum pudding this Christmas.... Only by our incessant efforts is the demand for infinite, or unrhythmical, change kept up.*
–C. S. Lewis

My successful engagement with life and with living requires me to live above circumstances—throwing myself into the processes of life whether struggling with cancer or on vacation in Yosemite.

I have been in a process of learning the wonderful truth behind this instruction's quote. The older and more experienced I become in the ways of heaven and earth, the more clearly I am "transported by," to use C.S. Lewis' term, the normal rhythms in life.

The blossoms of springtime lift my heart for many weeks. I deeply enjoy the segue of springtime bloom and blossom into summer fruit and leaf, then into beautiful and delicious fall harvests, then into the lively festivities of Halloween, Thanksgiving, and Christmas.

I relish the cadences of the individual weeks! On Monday morning I begin work with keen anticipation of the gifts that Heaven will send my way during the week ahead. I love the weekends and enjoy leisurely Saturday mornings with my wife, Sundays at church with my friends and my God, and popcorn on Sunday evenings.

Each day comes with rhythms that renew and bless my life. Morning workouts on my Wii Fit, a delicious cup of coffee, the pleasure of fellowship with my fellow-workers, a tasty lunch enjoyed with family or friends, afternoons full of satisfying work and cheerful banter with people who come into my life, the pleasures of dinner, enjoyment of ten pages of a good book in bed, and then falling into welcome sleep. How many times as I closed my eyes have I rejoiced in the realization that I had spent an entire day full of happy challenges and good people, without a single unpleasant moment in it!

My entire life has been a cycle that is analogous to a single day. During the early spring and summer periods, I experienced some tough weather. Now that I am in the midst of my autumn years, however, I have learned to appreciate the patterns with which my life seems to be continually blessed. The night of death is surely coming, but I am planning to experience my demise....

> *Like one who wraps the drapery of his couch*
> *About him, and lies down to pleasant dreams.*

... as master Bryant advised.

In this instruction's key quote, from C.S. Lewis' incomparable *Screwtape Letters*, the arch-demon, Screwtape, notes that joyful embracing of life would be the experience of everyone if they, the devils, were not diligent at their work. By the grace of Heaven, a wide space seems to have been cleared for me wherein I am sheltered from any dark or dysfunctional powers. I seem to be living my life in an extensive space in which the endless "novelty and familiarity" of existence becomes beautiful by the light of grace. My continual satisfaction reminds me of the words of my favorite hymn:

> *Mine is the sunlight! Mine is the morning*
> *Born of the one light Eden saw play.*
> *Praise with elation! Praise every morning*
> *God's recreation of the new day!*

I am so grateful that the cadences in my life—the daily, seasonal, quarterly, yearly, and decade-long rhythms—provide a never-failing source of fuel for my experience of joy. My whole life is a rock concert; I am up on my feet and I am dancing!

## Try This

1. *Resolve to embrace with joy each part of the day that comes to you throughout the next three days.*

2. *Open your eyes and the eyes of your heart to the seasonal beauties that surround you. Look for them! Enjoy them!*

# Day 20—Walk in Forgiveness

*Forgiveness does not always lead to a healed relationship. Some people are not capable of love, and it might be wise to let them go along with your anger. Wish them well, and let them go their way.* –Real Live Preacher

This instruction's key quote reveals an important obstacle that lies in the path of people who desire to put their whole selves into life. The problem can be noted in a famous paradox: We can do anything we wish to do except decide what it is that we are going to wish to do.

I have made a lot of mistakes. Some of them were wrong-headed—errors that I commit out of ignorance and stupidity. However, many of them were admittedly wrong-hearted—constituting actions that come from dark emotions such as anger, malice, intolerance, vengeance, and hatred. I have been able to correct the mistakes of the wrong-headed type through education, experience, and coming to wisdom; but mistakes based upon the darker emotions were more difficult to correct because they required a change of heart, which is a demanding and difficult transition.

The pressures for changing my heart came through the problems that the dark emotions continually create in hurt feelings, broken relationships, and lost opportunities for blessing others and receiving blessings. The challenge has been to put away the dark and evil parts of my nature. The American playwright August Wilson gave good advice when he said:

*Confront the dark parts of yourself, and work to banish them with illumination and forgiveness. Your willingness to wrestle with your demons will cause your angels to sing. Use the pain as fuel, as a reminder of your strength.*

Someone told me that the only prayer I need ever offer is to ask for forgiveness, because when I am forgiven, the restorative power of God then moves me into the position where I can receive everything I need in order to become happy, productive, and prosperous. Just as important as finding forgiveness—or more important, perhaps—is for me to come to the point where I forgive others. Forgive everybody! Forgive everything! Gordon Atkinson, the "Real Live Preacher," who wrote this instruction's key quote caught another important truth when he wrote,

> *It really doesn't matter if the person who hurt you deserves to be forgiven. Forgiveness is a gift you give yourself. You have things to do and you want to move on.*

C.S. Lewis correctly noted that, "Forgiving and being forgiven are two names for the same thing." In spite of any effort that I offer to try to get back in the good graces of angry people, they sometimes continue to be mad at me for one reason or another. Fortunately, my need for other people to forgive me is much less important than my need to forgive others. I can't control whether or not people will forgive me but I am in absolute control over whether or not I forgive them. How thankful I am that I can be forgiven whether or not individuals I have harmed are willing to forgive me. "Against you, you only, have I sinned and done what is evil in your sight," King David cried out (Psalm 51:4). Uriah, the man he had harmed by adultery, betrayal, and murder, wouldn't forgive him, of course, for a number of excellent reasons—the first one being that poor Uriah was dead. However, when David truly repented, he was made clean without Uriah's forgiveness. God forgave him with a cleansing that completely took care of David's problem.

During those times when God's forgiveness is all I can have, than God's forgiveness is all I need. "Forgiven people forgive people," so experiencing forgiveness at that level makes it even easier to forgive people who harm me in any way.

# Try This

1.  *Bring to your mind any angry unforgiving attitude that you have towards another person and by a deliberate act of your heart and mind, forgive the person sincerely.*

2.  *Think of someone who has some angry or harsh attitude towards you. Seek forgiveness from Heaven and don't let their feelings towards you influence your feelings about yourself. (Be sure to offer them whatever apologies or restitution you are able to make.)*

# Day 21—Be Excellent Towards Yourself and Others

*You train people how to treat you by how you treat yourself.*
*—Martin Rutte*

The most memorable line from the movie *Bill and Ted's Excellent Adventure* is the admonition that we should all "be excellent to one another." When I saw the movie, almost 20 years ago, I remember thinking that many religious people—including some preachers and theologians—would be better if they cast aside their weighty teachings and simply lived their lives according to Bill and Ted's simple principle.

My own liberation came about through completely disassociating my sense of self-worth from standards of behavior. I am free now to confess that I am a flawed person, but I have come to accept myself with all my wrinkles and warts—both physical and spiritual—because Heaven accepts me that way. I am excellent towards myself.

I still can't understand why I do some of the things that I do. I don't know why I can't take more control over my passions. Why can't I stop biting my fingernails, for example? Sometimes I think I am a little crazy. However, most of us feel that way at some level, if we will just admit it. Nevertheless, I am finally at the most healthy of all ego states, characterized by I AM NOT OKAY; YOU'RE NOT OKAY; BUT THAT'S OKAY.

My attitude is just the opposite of a quote I read recently: "I hate mankind, for I think myself one of the best of them, and I know how bad I am." Against that stands the magnificent observation by the writer, Anne Lamott—another person who sometimes seems insane:

> *Jesus' heart was not hardened against crazy people, or we*
> *would all be doomed. He was not embarrassed by craziness. He*
> *just said, "Yeah, well, me too," then he took care of you anyway.*

Through my freedom I now share at least one characteristic with people like Anne Lamott and Jesus Christ: We are safe. You can tell us anything. We will never withdraw in horror no matter what confession you make. We might cry with you but will never shame you. That reminds me of one of my favorite quotes by Anne Lamott:

# How to Put Your Whole Self In

*I did a lot of stuff before I got sober that I wouldn't do anymore. But there wasn't a single thing that I'd do that Jesus would say, "Forget it, you're out. I have had it with you, try Buddha!"*

It's only natural for me to love in the same way that I feel myself to be loved. If Heaven accepts me as I am then I would be both hypocritical and disingenuous to reject a single person. I have lost the ability to be critical about anybody.

*The Shack* is a bizarre book with some incredible insights. One of them was a comment by God Almighty—who appeared as a character in the book—that love doesn't expand; knowledge expands. In other words, the greater our knowledge of another person grows, the more about them we find to love. Everyone has amazing strengths and dismaying weaknesses. As I learn about the failures and successes of others, when my attitude is marked by a determination to excellence, my love for them expands to embrace both their shortcomings and victories.

Real love means coming to appreciate people *because of* who they are and not *in spite of* who they are. The most obvious course of action for me is to treat people "excellently," which will perhaps encourage them to treat others, including myself, in the same way.

# Try This

1. *Throughout the course of the next 24 hours treat with excellence every person you meet.*

2. *As you do so, watch how their attitude towards you becomes softer and friendlier. And watch how your attitude towards them and towards yourself becomes softer and friendlier, as well.*

# Day 22—Focus on the Present

*Are you so busy getting to the future that the present is reduced
to a means of getting there? Stress is caused by being 'here' but
wanting to be in the future. It's a split that tears you apart
inside.... The more you are focused on time—the past and
future—the more you miss the Now, the most precious thing
there is.... Always say "Yes" to the present moment.*
*—Eckhart Tolle*

I never have an anxious minute because several years ago I ran across a
piece of advice that instructed me never to worry about anything that I *could*
change, but to just go change it—then followed it up with another piece of
advice to never worry about anything I *couldn't* change because no amount of
worrying would help anyway. The advice contains what logicians refer to as
an "excluded middle"—a situation in which a matter could be one way or it
could be another but there was no middle ground between two choices. No
matter how bad any situation is I can either do something about it, or I can't
do anything about it. In either case, worrying is useless.

If I measure wealth by the quality of my life and by my enjoyment of
the things I do every day, then I am as wealthy as a king. An important part of
my enjoyment of life is my determination to never operate out of distracting
worry or enervating fears about the future. According to C.S. Lewis' *Screwtape
Letters*, focusing too desperately on the future would be to submit to the will
of demonic forces because, as one of the demons in the story said:

> *We want a whole race perpetually in pursuit of the rainbow's
> end, never honest, nor kind, nor happy now, but always using
> as mere fuel wherewith to heap the altar of the Future every
> real gift which is offered them in the Present.*

Focusing on the present and eliminating fears or even avoiding undue
expectations about the future frees me to make mistakes. "While one person
hesitates because he feels inferior," someone said, "the other is busy making
mistakes and becoming superior."

# How to Put Your Whole Self In

A healthy focus on present activities doesn't preclude appropriate planning or goal setting. I should have a clear view of where I am going with any activity. However, focusing on the present relieves me of the limitations that fear will always impose upon my actions and choices. "You are going to let the fear of poverty govern your life," someone said, "and your reward will be that you will eat, but you will not live.

We should leap whole-heartedly into our tasks, discounting our fears and confronting challenges with the same exuberance as displayed by the young rebel soldier in the Civil War who leaped out of his trench at the beginning of a battle, shouting at his comrades, "Let's go, boys! I am going to kill as many of them as they kill of me."

I continually feel like I am receiving the blessing promised by God, "Open your mouth wide and I will fill it." I open myself fully to the grace of Heaven and in return Heaven is filling my life with good things. Kahlil Gibran, the Lebanese poet and philosopher, attributed such a lifestyle as a quality of living life immersed in a love that "…has no desire but to fulfill itself. To melt and be like a running brook that sings its melody to the night. To wake at dawn with a winged heart and give thanks for another day of loving." Gibran got it right! That's just the way it feels!

# Try This

1.  *No matter what you do today or who you meet, throw yourself completely into every one of the tasks and into all the relationships.*

2.  *When you go to bed, spend a few moments reviewing the day and observing how the change of attitude added a quality of joy to working and being with others.*

# Day 23—Move into a Sun-filled Space

*You cannot go around and keep score. If you keep score on the good things and the bad things, you'll find out that you're a very miserable person. God gave man the ability to forget, which is one of the greatest attributes you have. Because if you remember everything that's happened to you, you generally remember that which is the most unfortunate.*
*–Hubert H. Humphrey*

Humphrey's wry comment resonates with my own experience. Like most people, I have had a difficult time coping with personal failures. It's always been a challenge to keep these from becoming defining events in my life; they tend to create the content of my attitudes toward myself. Keeping record of low and contemptible things I have done in the past inhibits me from performing up to my natural levels as a productive happy human being, which I believe to be the birthright of every human being. Joyful exuberance is the condition I will come to as I cease being turned aside by memories of negative personal experiences. This deliverance occurs by simply receiving the grace that comes following frank confrontation with the problem, and simply letting go—dropping the dreadful load at the Master's feet.

Wonderful things happen to me when I come into the sunshine through the entryway of discarded personal failures because dark things from the past lose their hold over me and I finally discover the "ability to forget" that Humphrey spoke about in this instruction's key quote.

Another great thing about coming to this happy state is that I am no longer greatly moved by others' opinions of me. My sense of well-being is not dependent upon the attitudes of anyone in the world. I am able to maintain Kipling's ideal that "all men count" with me, "but none too much."

An even more desirable byproduct of my coming to the place of letting go of my record of failures is an increased ability to relate positively to the people about me. Since I acknowledge my failures and shortcomings, but am no longer willing to let these things define me, my acceptance prevents me from defining other people by their own lapses, lacks, and limitations. I am no longer able to regard anybody with disdain but am willing to ignore any differences of opinion, conviction, or belief that I might have with others. I am preserving as an ideal Edwin Markham's great poem:

> *He drew a circle that shut me out*
> *Heretic, rebel, a thing to flout*
> *But love and I had the wit to win*
> *We drew a circle that drew him in*

For example, I no longer react out of my own libertarian bias to any liberal I meet. I won't respond from any disapproving heterosexual convictions I might have towards any gay person. I refuse to let my Protestant convictions stand between myself and any devout Catholic, Mormon, Jew, Muslim, or even atheist. I'll not permit my passionate conviction about the inclusive nature of the moral universe to interfere with my willingness to draw any judgmental fundamentalist into the circle of people I love and cherish. I finally understand in my heart that every liberal, homosexual, bigot, or devotee of any religion is infinitely greater than whatever label he/she bears.

I am no saint. My wife will attest to the fact that I can sometimes be as crabby or thoughtless as anybody. Nevertheless, life has a sunny tendency these days. Living requires less effort; I am not trying so hard anymore; I am learning just to "let it be." Since the doors to Heaven are open and I am being drenched in the sunlight that pours through them every day, I no longer even understand Humphrey's comment about "keeping score."

# Try This

1. *Write down on a piece of paper a short note about anything from your past that has been dragging you down and then burn the note in an ashtray. Resolve to regard any other failures or shortcomings you have as having been consumed in that same cleansing fire.*

2. *Treat the lapses of others with the same sense of release that you now have towards your own shortcomings. Neither you nor they will be defined by failure.*

# Day 24—Learn to Boost Others

*Treat people as if they are what they ought to be, and you help
them to become what they are capable of being.*
*—Johann von Goethe*

"If you would lift me up," Emerson said, "you must be on higher
ground. One of the greatest rewards for the "higher ground" I am on today is
the pleasure of helping others join me, which becomes the best part of putting
my whole self into relationship with others. In the words of an old proverb,
we actually help each other "as iron sharpens iron"—assisting one another in
reaching our potential for goodness and self-worth by the simple method of
treating one another as though each of us are valuable human beings. I will
get the best out of people by going to what is best in them.

A new grade school teacher was assigned a classroom of brilliant
students. She could tell from their reported IQ scores that hers was the most
gifted class she had ever heard of. Because of their extraordinary abilities, the
teacher devised special projects and assignments that would help the students
achieve their high potentials. The teacher found the class to be the best and
most rewarding group that she had ever taught!

One day in the teachers' lounge, so the story goes, the teacher overheard
a co-worker make a disparaging comment about one of the students from
the high-intelligence group, saying that the boy was incapable of learning.
"You must be kidding," the teacher remarked. "He is a gifted person. He's a
borderline genius."

The other teacher replied that the student was closer to being a moron
than a genius. The first teacher insisted that the boy was very bright and took
her colleague to see the scores for herself. She discovered to her amazement
that what she had taken for IQ scores were actually locker numbers.

That story gave me permission to treat others with the same grace that
I myself receive from Heaven, because I have come to believe that, rather than
observing my behavior and judging me for any mistake, God actually has the
kind of benevolent expectant attitude towards me illustrated by that teacher.

# How to Put Your Whole Self In

I've learned to relate to everyone as the teacher related to the children she was teaching. I'm surrounded by wonderful people! I have come to believe that part of the reason why the people around me are such extraordinary human beings is that I expect them to be excellent. Perhaps the power of positive expectations comes about because imagining that others are good gives them the courage to be so; treating them as though they can do good gives them the audacity to do so. They discover in my attitude a source of courage that enables them to live up to my expectations.

The African-American autobiographer and poet, Maya Angelou, saw the connection between courage and goodness: "Without courage, we cannot practice any other virtue with consistency. We can't be kind, true, merciful, generous, or honest." Our encouragement can instill the courage in others that Angelou describes.

I have learned to carry positive expectations into conflict situations. When people become angry and shout at me, I console myself with the idea that they are "just shrieking"—that their anger does not reflect their actual feelings; that they don't really mean their hot words. In every case, my positive attitude is rewarded by a return to cordial relationships.

I am so grateful that part of God's grace is to treat me as if I am what I ought to be! His acceptance of me helps me become what by His grace I am capable of being. Moreover, He gives me the ability to treat others as they deserve to be treated—each as a creative project that He is carrying out.

# Try This

1. *Look for some good trait in all the people you meet today and find something encouraging to say to them.*

2. *Note their reaction; see how many of them seem to appreciate and to draw courage from your comments.*

# Day 25—Make Blessings Count

*It's important to count your blessings, but it's more important to make them count. –Ziggy, Tom Wilson*

The little single-panel character, Ziggy, often looks forlornly out of his comic strip paper and pronounces some dismal observation about how life doesn't work as it should. In the case of the key quote in this instruction, however, Ziggy is shown entering a soup kitchen while making his profound observation about making blessings count.

The principle of using blessings to bless others is an essential one for anybody attempting to put his/her whole self into life. Counting my blessings is an effective method of acknowledging them as blessings. The great nineteenth century clergyman and reformer, Henry Ward Beecher, made an important observation:

> *I think half the troubles for which men go slouching in prayer to God are caused by their intolerable pride. Many of our cares are but a morbid way of looking at our privileges. We let our blessings get moldy, and then call them curses.*

The principle of blessings turning into curses is most obvious with material blessings. Some wealthy people regard their wealth as a burden—filling them with continual concern for conserving and maximizing their investments, weighing them down with concerns about the performance of the stock market or the state of the national economy. In some cases their palatial homes become sources of anxiety as they continually fret about maintenance, upkeep, remodels, insurance—and ongoing apprehension about whether some action of their neighbor or the government is diminishing the value of their property. The condition of these distressed wealthy people is made even more grim by their ignorance of the principle that they could be blessed much more by giving away their hoarded resources than by accruing them; that givers are more blessed through acts of giving than recipients are through acts of receiving—and much more blessed than are greedy people through taking, grasping, or stealing.

As a direct reversal of the phenomenon of good things exerting negative influences upon people with the wrong attitude, the act of embracing everything as coming from the hands of a benevolent God who does everything for my ultimate good creates blessings out of terrible things that come to me. The mystical Sufi philosopher and poet, Jelaluddin Rumi, wrote the haunting and provocative words:

> *I saw grief drinking a cup of sorrow and called out, "It tastes sweet, does it not?"*
> *"You've caught me," grief answered, "and you've ruined my business. How can I sell sorrow, when you know it's a blessing."*

"Count your blessings; name them one-by-one," runs the words of an old hymn. The wonderful advice points to a constant reality in everyone's life. In light of Ziggy's observation, I might paraphrase the song: "Check your blessings; share them one-by-one." We'll rejoice as we invest the recounting of each blessing from the viewpoint of generosity:

- I am blessed materially:
  Therefore, I tithe to my church and share with people in need.
- My life is filled with joy:
  Therefore, I try to share His joy with people around me who are hurting.
- I am filled with unshakable peace:
  Therefore, I try to be an emotional rock and a refuge to people around me who are shaken by life.
- The Master has given me a comfortable home:
  Therefore, I entertain friends and strangers whenever the opportunity arises.

What activity could be more happy than to keep counting my blessings? What better way to engage in life than by making my blessings count for others?

# Try This

1.  *List some of the ways that God is blessing your life.*

2.  *Consider how you might use one of these this week—or even today—to bless others.*

# Day 26—Set the Course of Your Life

*There are no whole truths; all truths are half-truths. It is*
*trying to treat them as whole truths that plays the devil.*
*–Alfred North Whitehead*

Part of my engagement with life is that I am able by the force of my will and the decisions that I make to determine the directions in which my life will go. This isn't a complete truth, but it is real. Someone said that we either force life to give us what we want or gratefully accept what life gives us.

Alfred North Whitehead, the source of this instruction's key quote, was a mathematician turned philosopher. His assertion that "there are no whole truths" is a little surprising since, as a mathematician, Whitehead certainly knew that some things are "whole truths." Math facts are absolutely true, for example: The truth that 2 + 2 = 4 stands above the vagaries of opinion, circumstance, and chance. Of course, from a purely logical point of view, there must be some things that are absolutely true or else Whitehead's assertion that there are no whole truths would itself become be one of the "whole truths" that he's denying the existence of.

(Coming back to the subject at hand…) The control that I exert over my life is one of the important half-truths that I remain conscious of as part of my whole-hearted engaging in life. Abraham Lincoln, himself, wrote, "I claim not to have controlled events, but confess plainly that events have controlled me." Even more true of me than of Lincoln, I have little power over the things that happen to me and even less over the outcomes of those events. For example, I may break my back, be unable to work, subsequently lose my house, and end up living in a dilapidated van in a seedy trailer court. That would seem like a failure. However, the accident might cause me to spend three years lying on my back in intense reflection resulting in my creating a work of literature that changes the world, plus bringing me great wealth and fame. Breaking my back, in that case, would have become an essential step towards a wonderful outcome.

On the other hand, I might start my own successful company, become a billionaire, and a year later fly my personal jet plane into a mountain. Becoming a successful businessperson in that case would have turned out to be an essential step in an awful tragedy. Accepting the limitations of my control over my life provides important protections against arrogance. I am *not* the master of my fate: I am *not* the captain of my soul.

Getting that out of the way feels good; it clears the decks so that I can assume an appropriate level of control over my life. The thing that I am actually in control of is not the outcome of my life but the direction in which my life goes. The elements in my life that are beyond my control are like the affects of weather and sea conditions on a sailboat in the middle of an ocean. The boat has no control over things like tides and winds but what the skipper does have control over is how the sails are set.

A poet named Ella Wheeler Wilcox made a compelling observation when she wrote:

> *One ship drives east, and another west*
> *With the self-same winds that blow;*
> *'Tis the set of the sails*
> *And not the gales*
> *That decides the way to go.*

The fact that I am in control of my life is a half-truth, as Whitehead would have admitted it to be. Nevertheless, the half that is true is a great truth indeed. By my beliefs, attitudes, and actions I really do profoundly influence the directions in which my life goes.

# Try This

1. *Reflect upon one direction in your life that you want to be moving towards.*

2. *Determine to change the "set of your sails" and move in that direction.*

# Day 27—Keep Calm in the Middle of Storms

*Never do anything when you are in a temper, for you will do everything wrong. –Baltasar Gracian*

Putting my whole self into my relationships with others provides a great protection against outbursts of temper or any show of ill will. Lashing out at someone in a fit of anger, of course, creates a diametrically opposite effect of becoming the blessing in his/her life that is my constant goal for every relationship that I am involved in.

Three hundred years ago Baltasar Gracian wrote a collection of sage advice bearing the wonderful title *The Art of Worldly Wisdom*. The key quote from this instruction comes from that collection. The caution against doing anything "in a temper" is important to everybody seeking to put their whole selves into life because Baltasar was right; when in a temper I end up doing everything wrong.

I have not always been perfectly calm. For example, I have had a problem with an irritable temper that bothered my wife for years. I have always realized that it does no good for my family or associates to see me out-of-sorts and listen to my bad-tempered remarks. I have never accomplished one good thing through any of my outbursts.

The Bible talks about the peace of God that "transcends all understanding" (Philippians 4:7). However, this kind of peace doesn't exceed understanding because it involves some complicated insight that is difficult to grasp, but because the peace surpasses expectations or explanations. I was amused by Helen Keller's response: "I do not want the peace that transcends understanding. I want the understanding that brings peace." I want that understanding also.

I once read the account of an airplane that experienced a terrible failure of some kind and began to plummet towards the ground. Passengers, of course, were screaming and crying out in fear and panic. One woman noticed that the man in the seat beside her was apparently enduring the experience with a calmness that was completely unruffled by the prospect of his approaching death. After the plane regained level flight and some measure of peace was restored, the woman turned to the man and asked him how he could have remained so calm through such a desperate experience. The man replied that he knew that he wouldn't die unless it was time for him to do so, and that a Divine Presence was with him in any case.

Of course, storms and turbulence are as much a part of my life as they are a part of nature. If peacefulness had only to do with easy circumstances, I would usually be living life with a very unsettled, troubled heart. The peace that "transcends understanding," therefore, conveys an ability to find a place of calm directly in the midst of any storm that might come blowing through.

The Bible compares the presence of God to a large rock that affords me with protection from whatever spiritual and emotional climates that I might find myself subject to. He is a refuge to which I can fly when the storms of life threaten to overthrow me. Whenever I need a place to fly to, He is…

> *A shade by day, defense by night*
> *A shelter in the time of storm*

… as the words of an old gospel song put it.

Because of His presence, deep within myself, right at the center of my being, there is a quiet place I can go to that cannot be disturbed no matter how fiercely the storms of life may blow around the edges—a calm sanctuary in the midst of any conflict or trouble. I do not always remain in that calm area, but the refuge is always available for me to fly to. And these days it is becoming natural and nearly habitual for me to go there when the angry billows of some tempest threaten to overwhelm me.

# Try This

1. *List several things that commonly make you upset and cause you to lose your temper. Reflect upon how pointless your show of temper was in each of these cases.*

2. *Seek the aid of Heaven in creating a place at the center of your spirit where you can find serenity in the face of conflict; peace in the midst of turmoil.*

# Day 28—Embrace the Future with Anticipation and Delight

*The Future ... something which everyone reaches at the rate of sixty minutes an hour, whatever he does whoever he is.*
–C. S. Lewis

People limit themselves and erect barriers obstructing the flow of good things that might otherwise come to them because they deliberately resist altering their patterns of thinking and behavior in order to accommodate the changes that are occurring in society.

In 1970 Alvin Toffler's best-selling book *Future Shock* focused on the reality that society is changing faster than some people can alter their understanding of society. As a result, according to Toffler, more and more people have a sense of their own culture being foreign to them—"future shock" becoming a strange form of culture shock. Not only is the world becoming a much different place than it was in the past, Toffler said, but the rate-of-change is itself speeding up.

I have witnessed greater changes in our society during the past ten years than during the three decades of 1954-1984. I have a cell phone with free nationwide roaming and long-distance, plus incorporating an appointment book, camera, games, a clock, a to-do list manager, and a database with hundreds of addresses and phone numbers—all contained in a device that is not much larger than a pack of cigarettes. No scientist in the world in 1974 could have imagined my phone. No layperson in 2000 could have imagined it.

I am always impressed by how technology lands on top of us, it seems, with no advanced fanfare. Microcomputers, video games, wireless phones, the Internet, cell phones, GPS, iPods, and iPads all came as a surprise; I never saw any of these things coming before they were announced in the media. I was amazed by VHS tapes, and never imagined how quickly DVDs would replace them, or that they, in turn, would so quickly become outdated by Blu-ray, and now by streaming media. It took radio 38 years to reach 50 million users but more than 100 million people joined Facebook in one nine-month period. Facebook has dramatically multiplied my own connections to family members, friends, and to the rest of the world.

# How to Put Your Whole Self In

I can't wait for the future to hurry up and get here! Science is making available for my enjoyment and growth more good things than I could take complete advantage of if there were ten of me!

Even more gratifying is the realization that the technology revolution is only beginning. What products and services will result from the current advances in studying the human genome, for example? Last year a company announced the successful test of two applications running on a quantum computer with processing elements comprised of individual atoms that one day will achieve computing speeds billions of times faster than today's super computers. What products will come out of that technology?

I could no more imagine the things coming in the future than anybody in 1974 could have imagined Facebook, or an iPhone. Three years from now I am going to be experiencing things that I can't even imagine today.

One hundred and twenty-five years ago, Robert Louis Stevenson wrote:

> *The world is so full*
> *of a number of things*
> *I am sure we should all*
> *be as happy as kings.*

My world today is full of things that Stevenson couldn't imagine. And we haven't see anything yet, because the future is coming on, as this instruction's key quote reminds us, at the rate of 60 minutes per hour. We can't change that or slow it down. I know this depresses many people and dismays more. However, I am putting my whole self into the changes that are coming. I am having a great time! My wish is to be amazed by all this stuff.

And I am!

## Try This

1. *Reflect upon the advantages of products you are using today that you couldn't have imagined a decade ago.*

2. *Determine to embrace and make use of new capabilities that are coming your way rather than ignoring them or letting them run over you.*

# Day 29—Hold on to Your Opinions with a Light Grip

*Opinion has caused more trouble on this little earth than plagues or earthquakes. —Voltaire*

For decades my opinions stood in the way of my efforts to be good for myself, good for others, and good for Heaven's sake. I would lose my sense of serenity, get into trouble with other people, and fall out of relationship with Heaven whenever I permitted opinions to create within my heart feelings of judgment, contempt, derision, and scorn for those who hold to opinions that differ from my own—or even towards those who simply don't wholeheartedly agree with me.

Based on our opinions about the existence of God or Allah, for example, or gay rights, taxes, racial differences, politics, abortion, evolution, hair styles, the Big Bang Theory, sports, (the list is unbounded), I could judge and condemn people "on the other side," thus cutting myself off from those who hold to contrary opinions from my own.

All too often, I have most strongly believed what I least understood. I used to believe that I could "prove" the existence of God, for example, but the belief required a certain degree of unawareness. Nobody who has taken a graduate course in philosophy believes that anybody can prove God's existence. It was impossible for anybody to convince me of error because nobody can defeat an ignorant person in an argument—and the hard reality is that from a purely rational position I didn't know very much. Still don't!

I know people who have never heard of John Maynard Keynes but who are sufficiently convinced of their grasp of economic theory to condemn President Obama's or President Bush's economic philosophies as being idiotic and evil. Some people who don't balance their checkbooks are enraged by Obama's unwillingness to conform his economic decisions to their own opinions about finance. Some protestors who couldn't locate Afghanistan on a world map take time off work to carry a placard in a rally against American policy in the Middle East. Others have rigid opinions about global warming even though they wouldn't know the Coriolis effect from the aurora borealis.

Since the opinions of such people aren't based upon any good information, they are merely expressions of the people's particular biases and, therefore, come under the sinister observation of an old Hebrew proverb that "Opinions founded on prejudice are always sustained with the greatest violence."

The more I learn, the less certainty I have about the things I believe to be so. The frontier philosopher, Ambrose Bierce, once defined "education" as "That which discloses to the wise and disguises from the foolish their lack of understanding."

"You can't believe everything you see," they say, but I made a great leap forward in wisdom when I finally learned that neither can I believe everything I think. When compared to all there is to know, I really don't know much. Therefore, I am always fighting the temptation to believe anything to be true just because it makes sense to me.

I am absolutely sold out to the presence of The Master in my life as the source of glue that holds my life together and that He works through me to accomplish whatever good I can in this world. Nevertheless, I am perfectly at ease in the presence of people holding to religious convictions that differ from my own. What proof do I have that I am right? How do I know they are wrong? By not having the slightest urge to harshly condemn, judge, criticize, or even argue with people, I am finally at the point at which I can actually love on them with my whole heart. What a relief it has been to come to this point!

Sometimes, when they come to realize the sincerity of my love, other people actually listen thoughtfully to the most important opinion in my life—the willingness and ability of The Master to bring good things out of bad.

## Try This

1.  *Take a fearless inventory of your worldview and note how little you believe that you could convincingly argue with a skeptic by rational proofs.*

2.  *For the next 24-hours don't get into pointless arguments with anybody. Don't condemn anybody. Simply demonstrate love to them in any way you can think of doing so. See what happens.*

# Day 30—Love Your Way into Health

*We must begin to love in order that we may not fall ill,*
*and we must fall ill if, in consequence of frustration, we*
*cannot love.* —Sigmund Freud

I put my whole self into life by engaging others from a perspective of unconditional love.

Something new came into my life when I read Freud's observation that is the key quote of this instruction. I had known for years that love is required from me by the demands of Heaven. I now have come to realize that I must have love in my heart because Freud says it is the only way to remain healthy. Perhaps Freud even connected loving to physical health. Scientists tell us that expressions of love release hormones that contribute to wellness.

Wretched people in this world fall into the illness that Freud refers to because they feel that the sources of their love have been withdrawn: lovers have left them, parents have abused them, friends have betrayed them.... They feel that they aren't being loved anymore but Freud would apparently say that their real problem, in fact, is that they have stopped loving.

Love that springs from grace has an indomitable quality. I am free because the inflow of kindness has filled me to the point that people cannot escape my love. They are able to withdraw so that my love can no longer affect them, but they are unable to do anything that would lesson my regard for them or cause my commitment to them to cease. Even the disdain that others might show towards me, although it is unpleasant, isn't complicated by any unhealthy sense of personal rejection or by reacting in hostility to the affront. My love for people who are themselves unloving and unlovable has an effortless quality because I am simply paying forward the love that I have myself received. I don't have to try to love them for who they are; I love them for what I have become.

Love begins with my family. My love for Rae, my wife, becomes less anxious and more healthy each year. I have become a one-woman man and that eliminates in a single stroke the difficulty, anger, and anxiety that otherwise would afflict me and drag me down. Years ago I read the following story on the Internet. I think it is true. The story makes me laugh and cry; it fills my heart with hope:

# How to Put Your Whole Self In

*A few years ago, at the Seattle Special Olympics, nine
contestants, all physically or mentally disabled, assembled at
the starting line for the 100-yard dash. At the gun, they all
started out, not exactly in a dash, but with a relish to run the
race to the finish and win. All, that is, except one little boy who
stumbled on the asphalt, tumbled over a couple of times, and
began to cry.*

*The other eight heard the boy cry. They slowed down and
looked back. Then they all turned around and went back.*

*Every one of them.*

*One girl with Down's Syndrome bent down and kissed
him and said: "This will make it better." Then all nine linked
arms and walked together to the finish line.*

*Everyone in the stadium stood, and the cheering went on
for several minutes.*

These children were engaging fully in life as they displayed this quality
of love for each other. In a similar way, love becomes a power within me
enabling me to do those things that make me a complete, psychologically
healthy human being. Such love provides the ability to eliminate the frustration
Freud talked about and, with complete health, to hold other people's hands on
the way towards the finish line. Every day! Today! What a wonderful way to
live! What a life! How healthy it feels!

# Try This

1. *Tell three people today, "I love you" to whom you have never
   said the words before. (Don't spoil the effect by telling them
   about this assignment!)*

2. *Observe the effect that deliberately loving on other people has
   on your own sense of wellness and joy.*

# Day 31—Become Habitually Excellent

*Habit rules the unreflecting herd. —William Wordsworth*

I am making it my goal to get in the habit of being successful. Every day I am working towards my dreams and goals. I get out of bed with my mind full of the things I am going to do that day in order to work towards my dreams. It's important to develop these habits. "We are what we repeatedly do," Aristotle said. He then drew an obvious conclusion. "Excellence, then, is not an act but a habit."

This hasn't come easily to me because I am a fundamentally shiftless individual. Most of my dreams have died because of the lack of follow-through. Rather than doing what I needed to do in order to accomplish the things that I wanted to have in my life, I would turn aside to the "unreflecting herd" habits that included such things as reading useless literature—thousands of pages that did nothing to improve myself or my place in the world and only little to actually entertain me. I've been guilty of watching untold hours of television programs that taught me nothing while failing to amuse me very much, and playing thousands of hours of electronic games trying to attain high scores that impressed nobody.

The best thing you could say about all those books, television, and games is that they provided diversion. For the most part, they kept me from being bored. However, that isn't enough. I don't want on my tombstone: HE WASN'T TOO BORED.

I am getting into the habit of doing things to make me successful, which means that I remain in contact with the people around me. My definition of success depends upon my being available to others—actually being for others what they need me to be. I can do things I don't feel like doing because I simply decide that I will do them.

One thing the people around me need most of all is my willingness to invest myself in their lives. If they come to realize that I am willing to put my whole self into my relation with them—that I enjoy being with them; that I enjoy serving them; that I'll be a shoulder for them to cry on and perhaps mix some of my tears with theirs; that I'll rejoice in their victories; that I'll be a true friend when they're needing a friend—then I can create a bond that will strengthen both the person I am serving as well as strengthening myself by acts of service.

I grow as I invest myself in others' lives; I put my whole self into the task of helping others become whole and thereby become whole myself. Here's what The Master said (following the Message Translation):

> Listen carefully to what I am saying—and be wary of the shrewd advice that tells you how to get ahead in the world on your own. Giving, not getting, is the way. Generosity begets generosity. Stinginess impoverishes.

Habitually giving myself into the lives of others is making me a successful human being. By that I mean that I have become a person who, when I look at myself in the mirror, can finally respect the person looking back at me. The guy in the mirror has become someone that I can sometimes admire; a person whom I at last enjoy being with. Success in relationship with others often opens the door for success in other less-important areas including monetary gain and professional advancement.

# Try This

1. *Make a chart with two columns. In the left column put down three kinds of reading materials, entertainment media, and other trivial pursuits that you are going to avoid or at least control. In the right column put down three ways you intend to make yourself accessible to others.*

2. *Each day for a week review your progress and reflect on the outcomes.*

# Day 32—Sing a Song of Silence

*The first virtue is to restrain the tongue; he approaches nearest to the gods who knows how to be silent, even though he is in the right. –Cato the Younger*

The virtue of silence plays an important role in engaging in the works of God and in the lives of people in the world around me. It is too easy to drown relationships beneath waves of speech, to kill genuine passion by thoughtless sentiment, to bury the tendrils of wisdom beneath half-baked opinions, and to destroy opportunities to bless by harmful pointless criticism. I have finally learned the value of restraining my tongue. For years I would begin every morning with a prayer, "Lord, keep your arm over my shoulder and your hand over my mouth." When I first found this prayer, I knew instantly that it was a good prayer for me.

The knowledge, acquired through many personal experiences, of how damaging my tongue can be is one of the factors that helps to keep my words fewer and sweeter these days. People have damaged me with their words, opening wounds on my soul that I still carry. Furthermore, I have damaged other people with my words—harmed them far beyond the ability of any healing powers I possess to undo the wrongs I have done.

Words are powerful—carrying the ability either to harm or to heal. A paraphrase of Jesus' words by The Message Translation carries an ominous warning:

> *Carelessly call a brother 'idiot!' and you just might find yourself hauled into court. Thoughtlessly yell 'stupid!' at a sister and you are on the brink of hellfire. The simple moral fact is that words kill (Matthew 5:21).*

The Bible further says:

> *If anyone considers himself religious and yet does not keep a tight rein on his tongue, he deceives himself and his religion is worthless (James 1:26).*

Again (from The Message Translation)...

> *It only takes a spark, remember, to set off a forest fire. A careless or wrongly placed word out of your mouth can do that. By our*

*speech we can ruin the world, turn harmony to chaos, throw
mud on a reputation, send the whole world up in smoke and
go up in smoke with it, smoke right from the pit of hell.
(James 3:5)*

A passage in the Hindu scriptures, the *Upanishads*, agrees with the
Bible on the superiority of quietness. "Better than if there were thousands of
meaningless words is one meaningful word that on hearing brings peace. The
*Bhagavad Gita*, which is one of the most important of the *Upanishads*, bear
witness of the virtue of peace and not speaking too much: "For those who
have attained the summit of union with the Lord, the path is stillness and
peace." The Bible says Psalm 4:4 "In your anger do not sin; when you are on
your beds, search your hearts and be silent."

I thank God that I often successfully avoid the temptation to pronounce
some assessment or judgment that doesn't do anything to improve a difficult
situation. When I restrain my speech, I am not really approaching "nearest to
the gods," as Cato put it in the key quote for this instruction. However, during
those times of restraint the presence of the Master is nearest to me, keeping
His "arm over my shoulder" and keeping His "hand over my mouth."

Moreover, sometimes, when I am at my best, He even manages to
make a song of my silence. That feels good! That's a success!

# Try This

1. *Look for opportunities today to practice silence; say less than
   you would otherwise be inclined to say.*

2. *Note the peaceful effects that your stillness exerts on
   your relationships.*

# Day 33—Think No Evil

*Believe nothing against another but on good authority; and
never report what may hurt another, unless it be a greater hurt
to some other to conceal it.* —William Penn

I appreciate the wisdom of the key quote for this instruction. We shouldn't believe an evil report about another person or especially pass it on ourselves unless we have a good basis for doing so. However, the older I grow and the more wisdom I acquire, the more willing I am to let people be wrong without my speaking about them to others even when I know "on good authority" how wrong they are.

I really am trying to never listen to gossip about another person unless I am either part of the problem or part of the solution and can do something to make the situation better. If neither of those things are true, then I am trying to just turn a deaf ear to any gossip about others—just as I wish people would simply ignore any gossip about me, no matter how juicy it might seem to them.

I am sometimes required to intervene in situations with a gentle rebuke when a reproof might encourage someone towards good. At other times, when an offense or a crime is current, I need to be willing to jump in and defend the victim to the extent I can. However, if neither such intervention is in order, then why not just keep the fact of the problem to myself? In fact, I don't even keep it to myself anymore. To the extent possible, I simply throw the knowledge away from my mind. After all, that's the way God accepts me. He has put my sin behind His back, the Bible says (Isaiah 38:17). So that's where I am going to put it for others.

I am determined to remove from my own heart those feelings of superiority, arrogance, and cruelty that make it even possible for me to enjoy people's failings and gossiping about them. Such things certainly serve to diminish as a human being the person I am talking about—and why would I ever wish to do that to anybody? I can't remember the last time I had an unforgiving spirit towards another person. I can hardly remember when I last needed even to forgive another person.

## How to Put Your Whole Self In

Gossiping about another diminishes me as a person. A wise person observed that great-minded people talk about ideas, people with mediocre minds talk about things, and small-minded people talk about people. I expand my mind as I embrace the realities of the universe by talking about lofty ideas; I reduce myself to petty and contemptible levels by talking in denigrating ways about other people.

Just as importantly, I restrict the quality of my relationship with other people by speaking ill of them. When I pass on salacious gossip that I have heard, then I necessarily reduced my ability to love the people and to receive their love. Since that's the case, I intend to do nothing whatsoever to diminish my capacity for loving others and receiving their love. I intend to not participate in gossiping.

I am not perfect about this; but when I put down another person by saying some pointlessly bad thing about them, or even listening to such a report, then I am being false to my convictions and to my intentions.

A grace from Heaven enables me to accept people the way I find them—the way I am, myself, accepted. It would be inappropriate to ever enjoy any opportunity of speaking ill of another person who might be in need of forgiveness.

# Try This

1. *The next time someone gives you some negative report about a person, counter that by saying something nice about the person being gossiped about.*

2. *When someone tells you about some disgraceful thing that another person has done, tell them something that you've done that was even worse.*

# DR. DONALD HUNTINGTON

# Part II

## Learn Practical Truths and Bits of Wisdom

*We build our personal philosophy of living and serving by becoming wiser in our choices and behaviors. The following set of instructions will provide insights and encouragement about how the world works. They will equip you for being good for yourself, others, and Heaven.*

# Day 34—Connect with the Source of Your Power

*It is not on what we spend the greatest amount of time that molds us the most, but whatever exerts the most power over us.*
*—Oswald Smith*

My life is filled each day by an unfailing source of energy empowering me for both psychic renewal and spiritual growth.

The truck under a float for the Standard Oil Company in the Tournament of Roses Parade once ran out of gas. The entire parade was held up until they could bring fuel for the stalled vehicle. That company had billions of gallons of gasoline but their truck had run out of gas. I have demonstrated the same failure in my own life and lacked sufficient power to avoid making choices that resulted in unintended, horrible outcomes. At times I have been powerless in spite of the fact that wonderful and unfailing resources of spiritual energy surround me.

What is it that exerts power over me and drains me of energy to live an abundant life? Our culture teaches us to look for subtle, external explanations of dysfunctional behaviors in such things as childhood experiences or personality disorders. Sometimes the adverse influence of education, family members, friends, and especially parents is thought to rob individuals of the ability to live positive lives. We seek for all kinds of ways to explain our wretched, unhappy behaviors and our miserable choices; we find explanations in things over which we exert no control and which we are, therefore, powerless to change. Our situation can become so helpless that sometimes the best thing we can imagine would be just to die and leave the whole disordered mess behind. Life requires expending positive energy and we have run out of gas.

We need a better source of power! And we have one! The tragedy of any of us coming to the kind of powerless condition I have described is that we are running out of energy in spite of the fact that the resources of the moral and spiritual universe—of Almighty God himself—are always at hand. The great thing I have come to understand is that we are all awash in a sea of grace. I have also come to believe that the grace of Heaven is like a divine infection. It's a socially transmitted disease; we catch it from each other.

# How to Put Your Whole Self In

"Too often we underestimate the power of a touch, a smile, a kind word, a listening ear, an honest compliment, or the smallest act of caring," Leo Buscaglia wrote, "all of which have the potential to turn a life around." Most people miss (I missed for years) the simple but powerful resource Buscaglia refers to: A dynamic moral potentiality surrounding us like a cloud. A powerful source of energy, renewal, and health that is both acquired and dispensed through our performing little gracious acts.

A power finally is being exerted within me that boosts me into the sun-filled life. One passage in The Message Translation puts it, revealing "unforced rhythms of grace (Matthew 11:28)" so I can "learn to live freely and lightly." This source of power is far greater than all the dark forces that had been bringing me down. It's a power within me greater that the dark forces trying to drain me. I am a little vehicle needing fuel and He is Standard Oil, with boundless resources for guiding my course and for blessing me through His Presence and especially through the people that come surging into my life every day. I am so grateful that I am connected today to these resources!

My life is full of people that lift me up and keep the fuel tanks of my life running over. I am back in the parade moved with the daily pomp and circumstance of life.

# Try This

1. *List the activities and especially the people upon whom you can rely for renewal and strength. Foster the relationships and activities that make you strong.*

2. *Reach out today for the resources of Heaven; they are all around you.*

# Day 35—Open Your Mind and Heart

*Though by whim, envy, or resentment led,*
*they damn those authors whom they never read.*
*(Charles Churchill)*

Highly opinionated people tend to dismiss with scorn ideas that they have never investigated. A Jewish friend of mine wouldn't let his children read C.S. Lewis' marvelous *Narnia* stories. He wasn't willing to test his attitudes about what he perceived to be the evil character of literature that he never read.

I was able to engage completely in the world around me only when I became open and genuinely inquisitive about ideas that I didn't agree with— or didn't yet agree with. Many of the people I attended church with as a child were good, kind, and intelligent. However, they entertained no doubts concerning the truthfulness of their opinions. In the war of Light against Darkness, for example, Charles Darwin belonged firmly on the side of Satan as far as everyone in my church was concerned.

One day I stumbled across an old volume of *The Origin of Species*. I'll never forget the shock that came to me when I discovered how orderly Darwin's approach to the world was; how carefully he worked; how clearly he reported on the phenomena that he had observed during his famous voyage on the Beagle. It turned out that the people who vilify Darwin commit Churchill's intellectual *faux pas* of damning an author whom they had never read. Any informed person might raise some objections to details from Darwin's hypothesis—I am raising some myself—but nobody could take issue with the quality of his work or the essential correctness of his conclusions.

President Kennedy observed that, "Too often we... enjoy the comfort of opinion without the discomfort of thought." The attractive thing about prejudice, bias, and all forms of intolerance, of course, is that such positions are comfortable—sparing us the discomfort of thinking deeply about the world; enabling us to avoid the pain that always comes from change and growth. However, I can only force people and ideas into pre-conceived pigeonholes by refusing to engage with them. My opinions about homosexuals changed completely when I actually became friends with some gay people. My attitude towards atheists changed when I actually got to know some atheists on a personal level. My attitude towards Mormons…. I could go on-and-on.

What actually happens to everyone who is widely-read, open to ideas, socially active, and even moderately intelligent is that we come to engage in "critical thinking"—which Wikipedia defines as "…the purposeful and reflective judgment about what to believe or what to do in response to observations, experience, verbal or written expressions, or arguments." I am following Lord Bacon's wise advice, "Read not to contradict and refute, nor to believe and take for granted, nor to find talk and discourse, but to weigh and consider." Critical thinking opens my mind and heart to good things, because I grow and change as I engage with ideas that are different than my own.

How wise Lord Bacon was about the way people should read! How irrational my Jewish buddy was in avoiding wonderful literature simply because it was not in accord with his preconceived notions! How foolish my Christian brothers and sisters were about Darwin without ever reading the seminal work against which they railed with such passion. I am no longer willing to challenge the accuracy of any theory or doctrine until I am able to understand the mindset and perspective of the people who adhere to it. Until reaching that point, the only wise response is to simply admit my ignorance— never rejecting any opinion simply because it is in disagreement with views that I already hold.

## Try This

1. *Read a book by some author or on some topic that you disagree with most.*

2. *Read to "weigh and consider." Open yourself to the possibility that you might learn from some ideas that contradict your own most cherished opinions.*

DR. DONALD HUNTINGTON

# Day 36—Embrace Sunrises and the Laughter of Children

*Contentment in life is determined in part by what a person anticipates from it. To a man ... who thought he would soon die quickly, everything takes on meaning—a sunrise or a walk in a park or the laughter of children. Suddenly, each small pleasure becomes precious. By contrast, those who believe life owes them a free ride are often discontent with its finest gifts.*
*–James Dobson*

Some of us throw ourselves wholeheartedly into acts of living only when pain, suffering, and loss reveal the emptiness of the half-hearted manner of life we have been living up to that point. Before he contracted ALS (Lou Gehrig's Disease) the great scientist, Steven Hawking, says he was in a state of depression. Nothing seemed worth doing, he said. Nothing had the power to challenge his attention. However, when the doctors told him he would likely die within two years, Hawking says that he began to pay attention to what was going on around him. Things like "a sunrise or a walk in a park or the laughter of children" began to seem precious to Hawking. He also began to become fully absorbed in his study of science, which he had previously engaged in as though it were an unsatisfying hobby.

How strange life is! How much different than could ever be predicted by a non-participating observer! Steven Hawking is suffering terribly from his condition, which has left his body totally paralyzed except for partial use of the fingers of one of his hands. Many people would conclude that life lived in those horrible circumstances would become wretched and meaningless—a living death. However, Hawking maintains that his disease awoke him to beauty and meaning. It was the disease, itself, that really roused him to awareness of the world and to a sense of contentment and anticipation. The awful disease lifted Hawking to levels of engagement in life that brought him the success and popularity that he so richly deserves.

A magnificent surmise finally begins to grow in our conscience that the most difficult challenges can become our most profitable experiences; that the experience of genuine quality in life always depends upon attitude and never upon circumstance.

Troubles are going to come to all of us whether or not we are willing for them to come. The happiest people are not those who have no problems, but are those who have encountered difficulties and even tragedies and have overcome them. They have leaped above the necessity of merely coping with conditions that are less than perfect, or horrible. Like Hawking, they have learned to use a problem as a springboard to a deeper, more fulfilling, and happier life than they lived before. These cheerful people have learned with the Irish novelist and songwriter, Samuel Lover, that "circumstances are the rulers of the weak; they are but the instruments of the wise."

We shouldn't imagine that we require trials and calamities in order to be happy. We can find good things in bad situations, but the actual reality, as C.S. Lewis pointed out, is that "whether for good or ill, one's inner state seems to have so little connection with the circumstances."

I enjoy peacefulness, harmony, and comfort as regular conditions of my life. I wish things could be even easier, that I had more money, and that people were easier to get along with. However, I can maintain peacefulness—or recover it, at least—to the extent that I have learned to maintain an attitude of peace and joy that do not depend for their existence upon external conditions or circumstances. I am living life on the level that Steven Hawking is living it. I am embracing every part of it so that everything, in fact, "...takes on meaning—a sunrise or a walk in a park or the laughter of children."

# Try This

1. *Notice today the blessings that lie in the everyday experiences of your life.*

2. *Stop and enjoy them for a moment; give thanks for some particular blessing.*

# Day 37—Bask in the Pink of Health; the Best of Times

*Refuse to be ill. Never tell people you are ill; never own it to yourself. Illness is one of those things which a man should resist on principle. –Edward George Bulwer-Lytton*

One of the evidences of remaining completely engaged in life is to become too busy and have too much fun to worry about circumstances in the world that I can't do anything about, or even to worry about the condition of my body. I heartily applaud Bulwer-Lytton's prescription for health in the key quote above and have practiced it myself for years.

Plato made the observation that, "Attention to health is life's greatest hindrance." He was right! I just don't have enough time to worry about whether I am starting to come down with something or wondering if I should engage in some preventive health measures. I am thankful every day for my good health. I may be dead of some dread disease by the time anyone reads this but, if so, I will have gone out by ignoring the condition as long as possible. Fretting about the state of my health—whether I am coming down with something or whether I should be dosing myself with some medicine or vitamin supplement…, now that would be a nightmarish way to live.

The other thing I refuse to be concerned about is the condition of the times I live in. Ralph Waldo Emerson made the profound observation, "This time, like all times, is a very good one, if we but know what to do with it." Emerson was able to say that even though he lived through the Civil War!

As with everything else in life, my response to such things as health and the condition of the world around me all comes down to my attitudes. Of course, terrible things are going on in this "veil of tears." Some day I will die—probably die hard. There are problems involving justice and the environment that I need to fight against. However, none of these evils has the power to overthrow my internal experience of joy and even delight. Heaven teaches me every day what "to do with" my time, to use terms from Emerson's quote.

# How to Put Your Whole Self In

Anybody brought by a time machine from Emerson's world into ours would think they had been transported to paradise. Things like indoor plumbing, modern hospitals, the Internet, air conditioning, air travel, the interstate highway system, malls, Walmarts, DVD players, and hi-definition TVs would seem to belong to some heavenly level of existence. What's wrong with us, that so often we are not able to receive with delight the wonderful gifts our technological society has given us? The problem—my problem—comes down to the fact that if my life is untouched by grace, I will be miserable even if I live in a time and place providing aspirin, the Internet, and flush toilets.

Helen Keller thoroughly enjoyed her life though she was both blind and deaf. My Grandmother Huntington laughed her way through cancer and terminal rheumatoid arthritis. Billy Graham maintains a smile on his face while dying of Parkinson's Disease. My friend, who was undergoing chemo for serious cancer, kept cheerfully working and playing in between the times he is in the bathroom throwing up. The Bible says that Jesus, himself, died "for the joy set before Him" (Hebrews 12:2).

I refuse to be concerned about my health. I am going to enjoy the good things that come to me as a citizen in America in the 21st Century—embracing the products of all this marvelous technology without making any sacrifice for them! I am in the pink of health living in the best of times. A principle of grace is infecting my attitudes in both of these areas.

# Try This

1. *Whenever you begin to worry about your health, look around you and make a mental note of five things that make your life pleasant.*

2. *"Count your many blessings; name them one by one."*

# Day 38—Realize That it Really Is a Wonderful Life

*I went about in pity for myself; and all the while a great wind*
*was blowing me across the heavens.*
*—Ojibwa saying*

By living life to the full and putting my whole self into acts and attitudes of loving service, I am able to reap a harvest of joy and happiness that comes from my awareness of the connections I make with the people around me.

In the beloved Christmas classic, *It's a Wonderful Life*, George Bailey, transitions from being a depressed, suicidal failure into a person who, with shouts of joy, went dashing to meet the men who were waiting to take him to jail. The profound change in George's attitude came about when he gained insight into what the world around him was really like, and especially when he realized the effects that had come about through his whole-hearted commitment to life and service for the people around him.

I once read a report indicating that only 20 percent of Americans are happy. This finding concurs with a wry definition for happiness proposed by the psychiatrist, Thomas Szasz:

*Happiness is an imaginary condition, formerly attributed*
*by the living to the dead, now usually attributed by adults to*
*children and by children to adults.*

Many of us Americans are quietly desperate because we search for fulfillment in outward circumstances, which fail to satisfy us no matter how good those outward circumstances become. We consistently ignore the fact that the orbits of our lives must be circling around other things than food, clothes, and entertainment or we will always feel that life is meaningless. Like George Bailey, when relatively minor things happen to us—such as losing our money and reputations, and perhaps going to jail—we become depressed and believe that life has become empty. The fact is, the circumstances of our lives have nothing to do with the quality of our lives.

Six weeks before he died, a reporter asked Elvis Presley, "Elvis, when you first started playing music, you said you wanted to be rich, famous and happy. Are you happy?" "I am lonely as hell," he replied. We might argue that two out of three isn't bad, and that a person like Elvis should be contented with wealth and fame. Nevertheless, I am sure in his more reflective moments, Elvis knew that of the three goals, he really did miss the most important one. The only reason anyone would ever wish to be rich and famous in the first place is because of the belief that wealth and fame would make the person happy. The fact is, as Elvis discovered, if you can't be happy without money and fame, then you will be unhappy with them, as well.

I am neither rich nor famous, but I am a happy person. I have discovered that the winds of grace that are blowing me through this world move me into good places. Happiness never comes as a reward for something I have done but only because of my putting myself into the position of receiving what the Universe, after all, offers as a gift. The way to true happiness, in my experience, is simply to let myself be blown into positive relationships. Such gusts also blow me in the direction of joy-filled relationships with my wife, children, friends, fellow-workers, my religious community, and members of my extended family—all of them becoming part of "a great wind blowing me across the heavens."

I am at my best when I am simply aware of the fact that the "great wind" is, in fact, blowing me; that in some wonderful way I am just along for the ride. And what a wonderful ride it is! How eagerly I look forward to the destination towards which the winds of this world are carrying me!

# Try This

1. *Create a list of the important people in your life.*

2. *Commit yourself to deriving happiness from serving others— beginning with the people on that list. See how wonderful your life then becomes.*

## Day 39—Avoid Cheap Pleasure

*Many a man thinks he is buying pleasure, when he is really selling himself to it. –Benjamin Franklin*

One effective method of engaging wholeheartedly into life is to indulge deeply in appropriate pleasures.

I first read Ben Franklin's quote while sitting on the 16th floor of one of the most lavish hotels in Reno, Nevada. Decades have intervened since that day, but I can still recall the view of the glorious snow-capped Sierras from the large picture window. Far below we could see the railroad tracks that had carried us from our Bay Area home, passing right through the majesty of those alpine-like summits. We had watched in rapt wonder through the window of the dome car as vistas of snow burdened Donner Pass, blazing in brilliant sunshine, passed beneath our gaze. We had gone to Reno to see a group of Irish dancers and were not disappointed by the show they put on for us! Their legs moved in a blur in perfect synchronization as they danced across the floor with exhilarating exuberance! We enjoyed every single minute of it. Even the work I did using the Internet connection in our hotel's room seemed fun and satisfying.

Not everyone around us was engaging with such satisfaction in the pleasures that life offers. In Reno's lavish casinos, you will always find some people who are surely "selling" themselves to pleasure, to use Ben Franklin's term. These bedraggled spirits have sat at the gaming machines far past the ability the machines possessed to provide any satisfaction. The remarkable thing about the jaded creatures you can always find in those casinos is the lack of pleasure the gamers apparently derive form their experience. In some cases their eyes have taken on a glassy zombie-like quality that is unrelieved even by the infrequent occasion of their winning.

These wretched people are completely oblivious to the Sierra Madres' ongoing majestic show. They never take slightest note of the storms and sunshine that chase each other through the mountains beyond the casino walls. The dancers in the next room leap about with no attention from those people bending over their machines. The higher emotions of delight, joyfulness, gratitude, even cheerfulness seem lost to them as hour-after-hour they pull the handles on the machines that no longer draw from them any response other than stupefied fascination.

Such scenes remind me of a terrible passage from C.S. Lewis' *Screwtape Letters*. In the passage the mentor devil, named Screwtape, gloated to the apprentice demon, Wormwood, that the most gratifying experience for devils from hell is to lure people to damnation by their own lusts and depravities while denying to them any sense of delight or even satisfaction from their degrading activities.

Whenever I consider the condition of these sad individuals, it is always wrong to be self-congratulatory. I have, myself, on countless occasions experienced what Solzhenitsyn described as, "the failing of human consciousness, deprived of its divine dimension." My failings came through other ways than sitting at a slot machine, but my methods of drowning out pleasure were no less effective than was theirs.

Practicing the disciplines of goodness, self-control, gentleness, etcetera sets me free to enjoy life to the full. Wonderful! Edmund Spenser asked the question, "What more felicity can fall to creature, than to enjoy delight with liberty?" Nothing!

# Try This

1.  *Make a list of the three major ways that you use your free time. Assign each a number from 1 to 5: "1" being "much pleasure"; "5" being "no pleasure."*

2.  *Re-evaluate your use of your free time. Quit spending time on those rated below three; begin to search for others that could become "1s."*

# Day 40—Learn Unforced Rhythms of Work and Repose

*We must learn to be still in the midst of activity and to be vibrantly alive in repose.* –Indira Ghandi

Developing healthy habits of fully and completely engaging in life provides excellent protection against the forces of monotony, world-weariness, and ennui. I can't remember the last time I was bored. As I became engaged in life I found the cycles of life going on around me to be increasingly more interesting; people were fascinating.

I was on a plane once with my wife and daughter waiting for final preparations to be made before taking off. "This is so boring," my daughter complained.

"I haven't been bored for years," I replied. "These days I just go into my mind. There are so many things in there to think about, play with, meditate on, recite.... Aging gives the gift to never be bored. Your mind becomes a garden of interesting activities. I wouldn't be young again for anything," I told her.

A middle-aged woman sitting in front of us looked over the back of her seat and laughingly said, "Isn't that the truth!"

"The cure for boredom is curiosity," Ellen Parr said. Then she added, "There is no cure for curiosity." Developing a mind that is always happily engaged has diminished my inclination to get panicky or as upset when things go terribly wrong. I can sometimes keep my head when those about me are losing theirs, as Kipling advised. During public meetings and group practices when people are yelling questions and orders at each other, and confusion reigns supreme, I often find myself just doing my part, contributing quietly when appropriate, and not being tempted to add to the noise and confusion.

My work becomes part of my serenity and provides an effective cure for boredom. These days I sit in the back row of chaotic or tedious meetings with my MacBook on my lap, happily writing away. I remain aware of what's happening and ready to contribute when an occasion to do so arises, but cheerfully uninvolved with any chaos.

# How to Put Your Whole Self In

I can remain in that positive ego state because of my relationship to my Master. The Message Translation of a passage from Matthew speaks volumes to my heart and life:

*Are you tired? Worn out? Burned out on religion? Come to me. Get away with me and you'll recover your life. I'll show you how to take a real rest. Walk with me and work with me— watch how I do it. Learn the unforced rhythms of grace. I won't lay anything heavy or ill-fitting on you. Keep company with me and you'll learn to live freely and lightly (Matthew 11:28).*

Whatever the actual cause of my cheerful attitude towards living and working, the fact remains that on many occasions I have been able to show that only a change of viewpoint is needed to convert a tiresome duty into an interesting opportunity. God's grace combines with the fact that I am finally growing up to make my own experience these days conform to Gandhi's key quote for this instruction. I often am "vibrantly alive in repose" and "still in the midst of activity." Such repose feels good.

I am grateful for the possibility of changing my life. I am so thankful that the unforced rhythms of work and repose mean that the change tends in an upward spiral towards joy and harmony rather than a downward spiral to dissatisfaction and sorrow.

# Try This

1. *At some point today take a new look at some routine task and deliberately find an attitude that will invest the task with significance and pleasure.*

2. *The next time you have a few moments repose, deliberately fill your mind with some ennobling imagination or pleasant reflection.*

# Day 41—Take Two-minute Vacations

*In diving to the bottom of pleasure we bring up more gravel than pearls.* —Honoré de Balzac

A small but unforgettable event occurred one beautiful fall day a number of years ago. A task of some kind called for me to walk between two buildings at the business complex where I worked at the time. A liquid amber tree clothed in gorgeous fall colors stood beside the door of one of the buildings. I stood briefly reveling in that wonderful tree, gave thanks for a world in which such beauty could exist, and then continued with my work.

Several hours later, it occurred to me that I had acquired a new depth of spirit since I was a young man because I had been able to enjoy with all my heart the brief glorious experience and then had been satisfied. When I was younger I would have longed to play hooky from work the rest of the day and commit acts of "diving to the bottom" of the intense pleasure that the colors of that tree had aroused in my heart by taking pictures of all the trees in the little park by my work or jumping in my car and driving through the mountains.

Years ago a wise man encouraged me to take "two-minute vacations." That was good advice! That's exactly what I did while standing before that tree. I now have experiences like that every day, it seems. It is important for me to continually renew my mind and my spirit—to have many "two-minute vacations" when I am simply filled with a sense of wonder or even elation at some item in my environment, mind, or memory.

I sometimes begin work at 3:30 in the morning; other times I work *until* 3 a.m. I never experience brownouts or boredom. One of the reasons for my vigor is the renewal through those small vacations. The quality of my whole-hearted engagement in life is given huge boosts by these brief disengagements. My "two-minute vacations" always have the effect of reviving my sense of optimism about myself and about the world around me.

These short intermissions seem to have certain childlike characteristics. I often feel the way that a colt kicking up its heels must feel. I enjoy the experiences with all my heart. Perhaps this hints at a reason why Jesus declared that the entrance into the Peaceable Kingdom is reserved for people who become like children. Maybe the way into that Place really is found only by those who maintain a capacity for wonder—for maintaining a feeling of humble uncertainty, and a fresh sense of always getting started about the real business of life.

A remarkable phenomenon is taking place in my life: every year for the past couple of decades I could honestly say, "I have never had a more fulfilled, more joyful time than I have had during this past year." And for more than a decade during that time I had no steady source of income.

There are many reasons for the steady increase of the joy and pleasure I take from life. I probably don't even understand some of them. Nevertheless, one contributing explanation doubtless lies in Balzac's quote. I have gradually been learning during many pleasant experiences in my life not to try "diving to the bottom of pleasure." I am thankful for the opportunity of enjoying pleasure in bits and pieces. I am grateful for the multitude of little "vacations" that I take from every day.

# Try This

1. *Schedule some times when you will simply stop what you are doing and spend some time reflecting on some truth or beauty that belongs to your world.*

2. *Begin to maintain an informal log of these small "vacations"—listing the date and time of each, plus some note to yourself about how the particular beauty or truth affected your spirit.*

# Day 42—Open Your Eyes to Surrounding Miracles

*There are only two ways to live your life. One is as though nothing is a miracle. The other is as though everything is a miracle. –Albert Einstein*

People who believe themselves to be immersed in miraculous events are able to insert themselves into their lives with far greater enthusiasm and even abandon than those who live as though the events of their lives were meaningless or chaotic.

I suspected for a long time that people who said things like "everything is a miracle," as Einstein does in this instruction's key quote, are merely expressing their belief that God never intervenes in special ways outside our normal space/time continuum. The older I get, however, the more I begin to regard my life as being the matrix of miracles, as Einstein apparently believed it to be. I see the hand of The Master in the lives of my family, through the affection of my friends, in the faces of the people I worship and work with, in the events taking place in my professional life....

The life of devotion I currently am living has opened my eyes both to heavenly interventions as well as to the activities of a Benevolent Universe working *in* me and occasionally even *through* me. The Bible accurately observes that "...we know that in all things God works for the good of those who love him..." (Romans 8:28). In other words, Heaven is working "in all things" in my life to bring me to a place planned for me. I have never been more convinced than I am now that this heavenly "work" is demonstrably taking place; new realities dazzle me every day. They surround me. Everything is a miracle!

"Things don't just happen—they're planned," somebody said. I have witnessed on countless occasions how events in my life that seemed negative or even tragic lead to wonderful outcomes. On many occasions, I came to realize that the negative event was necessary for the wonderful outcome to take place.

A man marooned on an island for many weeks had managed to build a rude shed out of twigs and branches to protect himself from the weather and to shelter the few fragments he had been able to collect. He had also started a fire that he kept going from day-to-day to provide warmth and to cook the few fish he was able to catch. One day the man noticed with horror a cloud of smoke billowing up from his small encampment. By the time he got there, the fire had completely consumed all the possessions he had in the world. The man was crushed by his terrible loss. For hours he sat in a morbidly depressed state, wondering whether he should go on with his life or just swim out to sea and end it all. Three sailors suddenly walked up to him. Only then did he notice a large vessel anchored just off shore. "Where did you come from?" he asked incredulously.

"We saw your signal fire," one of the sailors answered.

My life is like that. Each painful loss opens doorways to a blessed future. Cycles of pain and discomfort leading to blessing and peace have become foundational principles in my life. A miraculous fellowship of shared suffering occurs among people who completely embrace the negative experiences that come to us. I agree with Os Guinness who said, "We don't always know why, but we know why we trust God who knows why." Only with this kind of faith can I experience the miraculous growth and blessing that lies on the other side of any pain and loss.

# Try This

1.  *Reflect on the worst thing that happened in your life and then list three good things that resulted from that negative incident.*

2.  *Use the exercise as a source of permission for you to expect blessings and growth to come from everything that comes your way.*

# Day 43—Recycle Your Garbage

*A totally secure man ... knows how to take the garbage he was dealt in life and recycle it into energy. –Larry Titus*

When I first read the key quote for this instruction I was struck with a truth that I had never recognized before. I realized that the reason the "garbage" I was "dealt in life" formerly had power to harm me was precisely because I was insecure in my own feelings about myself. I am finally becoming one of the mature human beings who fully engage in the processes of life and are no longer forced to live according to the bad "scripts" and dreadful messages that we all receive throughout our lives. The psychotherapist, Anthony de Mello, was close to an important truth when he said,

> *There is only one cause of unhappiness: the false beliefs you have in your head, beliefs so widespread, so commonly held, that it never occurs to you to question them.*

No lesson is ever taught in public schools more thoroughly than the principle that you are what other people think you are. Messages and opinions that we encountered in school often determine the amount of anguish that we experience or the amount of vanity that we must deal with. The power of such messages derives from our delusion that the messages' content is real and that what others think is important. However, why should I care a fig about others' opinions? Some people think I am a stupid person, but what should that mean to me? Does that mean that, therefore, I am an ineffective human being? Others think I am brilliant (or at least they say they do). What does that mean? Does my supposed brilliance mean I am a good person?

I might buy into the message, for example, that I am mentally slow and, therefore, my lack of intelligence makes me a person who should not be valued, which would make me weak and joyless. Equally damaging is the message that if I am smart then having intelligence makes me, somehow, valuable. Accepting such a message could create an arrogant haughty spirit that would have the effect of actually limiting my worth to the people around me and to Heaven.

# How to Put Your Whole Self In

The people in the world who are most free are those fortunate individuals who aren't concerned about their reputations. However, most people—young and old alike—are ill equipped to experience that freedom. Nevertheless, I can take control of these inner voices. I am training myself to ignore internal communications that drag me down. I create within myself a chorus of voices supplying positive messages that actually build up my spirit and encourage me to engage in those pursuits that positively impact my own live and the lives of those around me.

Dr. Seuss hit a nail on the head when he wrote, "Be who you are and say what you feel, because those who mind don't matter and those who matter don't mind." How wonderful it is to actually live like that! I am willing to consider other people's opinions of me, but am no longer willing to be defined by them.

The inescapable reality is that not until I can perform a deed of service with absolutely no regard for what recipients will think of me as the giver, am I really free to do good to them as an act of genuine love. Recycling the garbage of other people's perceptions into powerful and affirming attitudes and actions provides me with a basis from which I can be a positive influence in the world about me and in the lives of other people!

# Try This

1.  *Write on a sheet of paper, "Other people think that I am_____." Fill in the blank with a negative perception that you imagine them to have. For example, you might write, "Other people think that I lack good judgment." Now write the reversal of the perception. For example, "I am a person of good judgment."*

2.  *Your mind creates the reality in which you live. Determine to view yourself in light of the reversal of the negative perception.*

# Day 44—Be a Potato

*A man who has not suffered, what does he know? –Henry Suso*

Our engagement with life and with living is energized and vitalized by suffering. "Show me a person who has never suffered a loss," a clinical psychologist said, "and I will show you a person who has not evolved at all."

The encyclopedia says that Henry Suso, the source of this instruction's quote, "... was broken by hardships, persecutions, and slander." In response he wrote the *Little Book of Eternal Wisdom* and the *Little Book of Truth*. Suso would probably be able to affirm that sufferings had guided him to the "eternal wisdom" and "truth" about which he wrote. I read a stirring account in an issue of *Guidepost Magazine*:

> While my husband Frank and I were living in Pakistan many years ago, our six-month-old baby died. An old Punjabi who heard of our grief came to comfort us. "A tragedy like this is similar to being plunged into boiling water," he explained. "If you are an egg, your affliction will make you hard-boiled and unresponsive. If you are a potato, you will emerge soft and pliable, resilient and adaptable."

There's a vast difference between what I think is good and what is actually good for me. If I could control my circumstances, I would be enormously wealthy with unfailing good health. Nobody I knew would ever grow ill or die. Everyone would be loving and kind. Nobody would gossip about me or treat me with anything but kindness and deference. Everybody would admire and honor me. The Master knows that if I really could live life like that, however, I would probably become a self-important, conceited hypocrite. I must learn patience, humility, compassion, and sensitivity to others' needs. I must learn to be a person of deliberate prayer and meditation—conscious always of my dependence upon my Creator.

The annoying reality is that I only discover the power of love when I am in a situation that could make me hate, only learn to pardon by being injured, only learn real faith when faced with great doubt, only learn real hope in the face of despair, real light in the face of darkness, ultimate joy only after sadness, and real understanding after great confusion. Only personal troubles will really develop my patience. Personal failure is the soil in which my humility can grow strong. Pain and suffering are the experiences that develop my sense of compassion and sensitivity. The Master uses times of trouble to soften me so that He can mold my soul into the shape of His will.

The death of my 13-year-old brother-in-law, Rodney, created a sense of loss that can bring tears to my eyes even four decades after the fact. However, through that loss we all discovered by experience that we were held by hands that would never drop us. How else could we learn that? Going through cancer and the death of loved ones brought pain and even anguish to my heart, but they also provided energy for climbing to heights that I had not attained to before. Good health acquires a deeper significance following a life-threatening illness. Belief in heaven has a more profound dimension when the believer's mother is there.

I have no martyr complex. I pray all the time that The Master will hold back dark times from me and from those I love, but my hand is in His for whatever is going to happen in this world. If the worse comes, "O Lord, let me be a potato!"

# Try This

1.   *Reflect on the worse thing that has happened to you in the past five years.*

2.   *Identify at least two good things that came as a result of that pain.*

# Day 45—Eliminate Negative Attitudes

*When you look for the bad in people, expecting to find it.... you surely will. –Benjamin Franklin*

I am increasingly more troubled by the hostile attitude displayed by many people against those with whom they disagree. Some of us can become enraged at the drop of a hat. Moreover, as a friend of mine likes to put it, we carry around a large box of hats.

Nothing is more common than being contrary. No matter what anybody tries to do, a group of protestors will band together to oppose it. The angry people might be atheists or pastors, homemakers or harlots, but they share the quality of unrestrained fury. They "are mad as heck and aren't going to take it any more," to paraphrase a famous line from a movie.

The Bible says, "An angry man stirs up dissension, and a hot-tempered one commits many sins" (Proverbs 29:22) Then turns it around, "Hatred stirs up dissension, but love covers over all wrongs." Buddha agrees with the Bible about anger's bad effects. "Never in this world can hatred be stilled by hatred," Buddha said, "it will be stilled only by non-hatred—this is the law Eternal." If by "non-hatred" Buddha meant "love," then he got the matter exactly right. A spirit of criticism and a spirit of serenity, like oil and water, will never mix. I am challenged and rebuked by the words of Aristotle:

> It is easy to fly into a passion—anybody can do that
> But to be angry with the right person
> to the right extent
> and at the right time
> and with the right object
> and in the right way
> that is not easy, and it is not everyone who can do it.

I am one of the people Aristotle wrote about who lacks the ability to get my anger "right." Things surely are going on in our culture that I don't approve of, and that I work against and vote against. However, one of the things in my own heart that I work against are the feelings of hostility and the judgmental attitudes that my disapproval always tries to create. I have come to realize that none of my angry ringing denouncements in the past ever accomplished one bit of good. They always pulled down my own spirit and exerted a negative effect upon the people around me. I have proved on many occasions the truth of the Bible's assertion that "the wrath of man does not promote the righteousness of God" (James 1:20).

I have finally learned to forgive people for their offenses even when they don't deserve my forgiveness (very often they do not), simply because I need a forgiving spirit for the sake of my own inner weather. Someone named Hannah More was correct when she wrote, "Forgiveness is the economy of the heart..... Forgiveness saves the expense of anger, the cost of hatred, the waste of spirits."

Another awful outcome of negative thinking is that it actually brings out the worst in the people I am criticizing, as Franklin said in the key quote for this instruction. I am going to look for the good in people I meet however difficult the search may be, because that is the only way that they will ever permit me to engage fully in their lives.

How much more positive will be my effect upon the people around me if I approach the worst of them as though they were honorable, worthy human beings! They might eventually come to trust me enough to be willing to receive suggestions from me for changing their attitudes and behaviors.

# Try This

1. *Perform some gentle service to somebody you have been critical of.*

2. *Afterwards note the difference that your transformed attitude and behavior makes in your relationship with that person.*

# Day 46—Keep Your Feet on an Upward Path

*Sorrow looks back, Worry looks around, But faith looks up!*
*Live simply, love generously, care deeply, speak kindly, and*
*trust in our Creator who loves us. —Anonymous*

The quote for this instruction advocates four important goals for me as I seek to put my whole self into life and into living. A great deal in life depends upon focusing upon living simply, loving generously, caring deeply, speaking kindly, and trusting in my Creator because these activities constitute the mental and spiritual environment that both creates and supports a life that is lived large.

I read of a man who once found a five dollar bill lying on the ground and, according to the story, he never saw the sun again. I have been like that at times in my life—with my eyes cast down looking for some grubby profit or gain that, even if it came to me, would neither make me a better person nor improve my relationship to others.

These days I am looking up. My focus is upon people around me and upon Heaven above. I am trying to live so that my conduct and attitude would win Einstein's approval, because he said, "He who can no longer pause to wonder and stand rapt in awe, is as good as dead; his eyes are closed." Simplicity, love, concern, kindliness, and trust spring most naturally from a heart filled with the wonder and awe that Einstein was speaking about. Oswald Chambers, wrote, "We have to be exceptional in the ordinary things of life, and holy on the ordinary streets, among ordinary people." Then he adds an important caveat: "…and this is not learned in five minutes."

The Upward Path that I intend always to keep walking on consists of identifying the presence of The Source of direction and strength in my life and then committing myself daily to the divine will and plan as they become clear to me. An important part of this has been for me to make it a daily habit to practice the things that belong to a life of moral freedom—especially in deliberate reflection upon scriptures and upon the writings of gifted people. Every day I revise the daily reading in my online *Daybook of a Man Awash in Grace.* The routine becomes the way for me to focus my heart and mind on the things that help me be "holy on the ordinary streets, among ordinary people," as Chamber's quote says I ought.

## How to Put Your Whole Self In

Such regular exercising of my spirit strengthens my inner person, just as regular physical exercise strengthens my body. I am especially thankful for the relative lack of struggle and conflict in my heart as God gives me peace and joy as a gift. I have (finally) learned how to receive the gift and every day to spill it over to others.

I recently read of a wise mother who, when tucking in her children at night, would ask the question, "Where did you see God today?" They would answer by recounting the experiences of the day. I desire that grace might impel my life so that if those children had encountered me, they might tell their mom, "I saw Jesus in the thing that Don did." What in life could ever be more wonderful than that people could just "see" something about Jesus when they run into me? How willingly would I even suffer to bring that about! How gladly will I do whatever "good works" of kindness and love for any lonely people that Heaven sends into my path today!

Sharing positive passions with others is the best part of the Upward Path that I am walking these days.

# Try This

1.  *Decide that today you will not do one thing except those actions that not directly or indirectly maintain your feet on an Upward Path.*

2.  *Conduct yourself today so that someone might imagine, after being in your presence, that they saw God in you.*

# Day 47—Be Willing to Be Dazzled

*The truth must dazzle gradually*
*Or every man be blind. —Emily Dickinson*

Dickinson is right to some extent. The truth about the nature of life has been dawning upon me gradually for a number of years now, and I am still dazzled by it. The fact is that I feel like I started out blind and have gradually been gaining my eyesight.

Nothing in the world exists in a vacuum or has an objective identity that I can make out. As far as I am concerned, everything I encounter exists as an extension of the definitions I bring to the particular object or person— drawn from past experiences and connections that I have made with other things or people of the same type, expectations, fears....

For example, a long and almost completely subconscious list of experiences serves to inform and give structure to my understanding of the word "tree." The blazing fall colors of trees during my Pennsylvania upbringing, the orange tree in my back yard, and Joyce Kilmer's sonorous words about the tree that "looks at God all day and lifts its leafy arms to pray" would create a mental and emotional context of the word in a way that would be far different than if I had been a logger or a tree surgeon.

Since we relate to elements in the real world with imaginations fired by attitudes, perceptions, and experiences, I have begun deliberately to shape my imagination to the service of Heaven and of others. "Don't use your imagination to scare yourself to death," someone said. "But to inspire yourself to life." That is what I am doing. I am looking at the world with new eyes deliberately using my imagination to recognize the gifts that the Universe has scattered about me. In doing so, I am apparently following the lead of Einstein, who wrote:

> *When I examine myself and my methods of thought, I come*
> *close to the conclusion that the gift of fantasy has meant more*
> *to me than my talent for absorbing positive knowledge.*

Because I am now using my own "gift of fantasy," the world unfolds about me each day in a new and wonderful fashion. I now notice great gifts that were formerly obscured by an imagination mired in pragmatism and literalism. I find inspiration in small things that would be overlooked by a heart not prepared to be astonished:

- My wife loves to blow bubbles. Sometimes she carries them around her neck in a little vial and might blow them at any time. She laughs like a delighted child as she watches them float to the ground.
- The peace of The Master was in my heart during the decade that I was out of work with no regular income.
- My son enjoys spending time with me and playing his CDs, giving me lessons designed to help me share in his passionate love for music.
- My grandchild throws his head back and laughs out loud at every excuse.
- My daughter loves her life—her wonderful husband, her parents, her pets....
- My friends cherish me and receive my love.

It would be possible for these things to pass me by completely unnoticed. In fact, they often did pass me by before I had sufficiently clear imagination to notice the blessings that were in my life. My life is daily filled with moments when I feel like Scrooge waking up on Christmas morning. "I am as light as a feather, I am as happy as an angel, I am as merry as a schoolboy." My attitude shouldn't come as a surprise. After all, "Joy is the serious business of heaven," as C.S. Lewis said. So why should I be amazed when The Master performs His "business" in the life of one who is ready to be an instrument of His peace?

# Try This

1.  *For the next several days adopt a child-like attitude towards life. Set yourself deliberately to be willing to be dazzled by people and circumstances.*

2.  *Give yourself over to joyfully receiving all the gifts of life.*

# Day 48—Regard Life as a Learning Center or Dance Studio

*If you think of this world as a place intended simply for our happiness, you find it quite intolerable: think of it as a place of training and correction and it's not so bad. —C.S. Lewis*

The quote by C.S. Lewis points to one of the best possible attitudes for people who intend to put their whole selves into their lives. We could re-write "Shakespeare's Midsummer Night's Dream" to capture the thought, perhaps:

> *All the world's a Learning Center;*
> *And all the men and women merely students.*
> *They have their graduations and their kindergartens;*
> *And one man in his time passes through many classrooms.*

According to this vision, I can live life as though the hours of the day constitute a playground or a workshop in which I play or work as I choose. However, in my more serious times of reflection I realize that the hours of this day in reality constitute a lecture hall or a lab in which Heaven is trying to teach me lessons about grace, and is preparing me for eternity. It is to my advantage to apply myself diligently to the learning; to strive to prepare for the final exam awaiting me on whatever Judgment Day lies at the end of my path.

I will go into the world tomorrow morning with the idea that in some fashion I am being trained and tested for some unimaginably wonderful future. That attitude will then transform the quality of my experiences during the entire day. I am convinced that everything that happens in the sometimes-rough schoolhouse of my life becomes a learning experience. I am practicing a shining principle that Ralph Waldo Emerson described:

> *When a man is pushed, tormented, defeated, he has a chance to learn something; he has been put on his wits; on his manhood; he has gained the facts; learns his ignorance; is cured of the insanity of conceit; has got moderation and real skill.*

# How to Put Your Whole Self In

Learning can seem to be drudgery, but one way to picture the experience is to imagine life as a dance studio and that I am learning to dance. In the midst of life's storms, I am learning to dance in the rain.

"Dancing in the rain isn't something that most of us are born knowing how to do," the author B.J. Gallagher wrote, "We learn it. We learn it from others; we learn it from Life." And then she added a final, hopeful note: "The more we dance, the better we get at it." Living life at this level takes on a quality that some around us cannot comprehend. People who are unable or unwilling to hear the music that surrounds us like an ethereal light tend to regard our dancing as delusion or insanity.

Like actual dance classes, learning to dance to the rhythms of life involves discipline and energy—sometimes sweat and pain. The popular culture surrounding me doesn't assist me with my dance lessons. Such things as schedules, to do lists, and various media work to mitigate any type of sustained reflection or meditation. A continual blurring and buzzing confusion reduces the possibility of establishing internal tranquility.

Every day I am learning to shut out noise that interferes with my ability to hear the music of the spheres so that I can join in the cosmic dance. I admit that I am a slow student, often clumsy and unable in many cases to get the steps right even after many times of practice. However, I am finally learning the rhythms of grace that the Head Dance Instructor is trying gently to seal in my heart.

# Try This

1. *Start a journal; record each significant experience, whether good or bad, to see what you can learn.*

2. *Make a list of the lessons learned. Eliminate those experiences that contain no important learning; focus upon the ones that encouraged you to dance.*

# Day 49—Bury Your Hurts

*You have to dig deep to bury your Daddy.* —Proverb

My early attempts to engage positively with life were seriously hampered by events and circumstances that wounded me and prevented me from completely embracing the life around me.

My father died when I was 14 years old, and I am thankful that I have finally "buried" him. He was hanging around the edges of my life from early childhood even though I have no personal memories of the man. He left my mom and her three small children when I was four years old. I can remember a few scenes in which he was present, but I have no memory of his appearance whatsoever. I realized a few years ago how strange is the absence of my father from my memories. I remember my aunt taking me to the airport to see Dad off after my grandpa's funeral. I was probably five at the time. I remember actually going onto the plane for a few moments. I remember my aunt and me standing on the boarding ramp. However, every place where the figure of my father should have been in those memories is blank. I apparently deleted from my memories a person who was too painful to recall.

Dad never came back. He died ten years later without so much as an intervening phone call.

For years I had a difficult time burying that guy. I was a miserable little boy—a terrible student, and a strange, unpopular young person. Only when I got into my late 20s did I realize that my problems in making social adjustments perhaps derived from my inability to cope with the absence of my father. His ghost was probably hanging around, messing me up in countless ways.

I think that people like me who are marred by dysfunctional childhood influences learn to play games in order to prop up a slumping sense of worth. I grew up in a fundamentalist environment and we played a mean-spirited game in which we imagined ourselves to be part of a small pool of redeemed people surrounded by a great sea of people who were definitely not okay. It is amazing, in retrospect, how it was possible for me to be such a deficient human being myself and yet, for example, to feel superior to a doctor who had given his life in service for poor people in Africa if he had a brandy sometimes at the end of the day.

# How to Put Your Whole Self In

During my coming to a healthy embrace of life, I have learned not to merely accept people, but to embrace and admire them. I will be the friend of anyone who will permit me to do so. Norman Vincent Peale told us to, "Throw your heart over the fence and the rest will follow." I discovered that he was right because I have been throwing my heart over fences these days and finding deep satisfaction in the efforts.

I don't know if the realization that my father was the source of my problems (if in fact he really was the source) ever helped me in any way. However, by opening my heart to other people I have become a happy person leading a blessed life. The love of my wife and children, the warm fellowship of a great number of people whom I love and who love me including the people I work with, people I worship with, fellow members in my Rotary club.... These all come together with spiritual shovels in their hands helping me to finally bury my dad.

Grace has come into my life through a variety of channels, bringing me peace and happiness, together with a Divine Presence to take the place of that great wounding absence in my life.

# Try This

1.   *Take time for serious reflection about some person or circumstance that wounded you, possibly years ago.*

2.   *By a deliberate act of your will, bury that person or circumstance beneath a layer of grace that you receive from people who love and support you—while remembering "the everlasting arms" that are holding you.*

# Day 50—Take Your Stand on Giant Shoulders

*A dwarf on a giant's shoulders sees farther of the two.*
–George Herbert

I can only throw my whole self into life by understanding that I alone am responsible for my own success or failure. At any particular moment I am creating my own reality through choices I make. My destiny is a matter of choice rather than chance.

Only by being aware of my control over my destiny can I rise to become master of my circumstances rather than becoming victimized by them. Nevertheless, I am not exercising that control with any Lone Ranger-type independence because I am immersed in and bolstered by wisdom and teachings from an unbounded variety of sources—including magnificent ideas from great people who have gone before. As noted above in George Herbert's key quote, I have a breathtaking view of the unbounded possibilities of the world because I am standing on giant shoulders.

I am aware of the essential role that other people's wisdom and examples play in embracing life. Every day I am often astounded by the wisdom of others—always prepared to learn from them the insights, perspectives, and cautions that might steer my own attitudes and actions in profitable directions. I remain keenly aware that whatever wisdom and knowledge I possess derives from my reflection upon the tremendous network—the vast cosmic Web—of people who have brought me to this place.

Leo Stein (Gertrude's brother) made a perceptive observation that describes my attitude: "The wise man questions the wisdom of others because he questions his own, the foolish man, because it is different from his own." I maintain a level of skepticism that protects me from receiving anything merely at face value. I learned not to believe everything I think. Nevertheless, every day strong currents of true wisdom pass through the filter of my skepticism. I am continually lifted by the intelligence and understanding of other people.

Consciousness of the debt I owe to others becomes joyful realization as I embrace life with both arms. Rather than imagining that mine is a solo part; the little tune of my life becomes part of a vast choral production that the Universe has been singing since our primitive ancestors first looked up towards the heavens and began to realize that their lives were part of a symphony directed by some Cosmic Composer. The performance has since been carried along by the voice of every individual. The song of my own life blends with the voices of innumerable performers.

I have deep sadness for people who struggle through the years of their lives as an independent effort. They keep their heads down and their ears closed to the music of the spheres that is continually being created all around them. The tragedy of missing their place in the cosmic production has apparently been the condition of a majority of Americans for as long as there have been Americans. More than two centuries ago Thoreau made his dismal observation that "The mass of men lead lives of quiet desperation and go to the grave with the song still in them."

By offering my whole self as a sacrifice to God, He assists me in finding the right notes causing my song to blend in with the other performers in the concert. Returning to the original metaphor: God helps me to balance on the shoulders of wise giants who have gone before and to view the world from the lofty heights to which their accumulated wisdom has raised me.

# Try This

1.   *For the next week limit your reading to books and articles containing information and wisdom of the sort that will elevate you to a place where you gain a more unobstructed view of the world around you.*

2.   *For a week limit your television watching to shows that will assist you in making the choices that will set your destiny.*

# Day 51—Minimize Religion

*A religious man is a person who holds God and man in one thought at one time, at all times, who suffers harm done to others, whose greatest passion is compassion, whose greatest strength is love and defiance of despair. –Abraham J. Heschel*

In this instruction's key quote, the noted rabbi and theologian, Abraham J. Heschel manages to capture in a single sentence the essence of becoming good for myself, good for others, and good for heaven's sake. I appreciate Heschel's stipulated definition of "religion" as having to do with attitude and relationship rather than with doctrine or dogma.

According to Heschel's definition, some people aren't actually religious who go to church every week. We have true humility—except that we sometimes are filled with pride. We have perfect tolerance—except that we sometimes pronounce harsh judgments upon others. We are the most kindly of all people—except that we are sometimes indifferent to the suffering of others. We are the most authentic people—except that we sometimes play the role of hypocrite. We are filled with love—except that we sometimes harbor hatred in our hearts.

Christians have a reputation of being angry judgmental people and we sometimes richly deserve the reputation. Voltaire wrote, "Of all religions, the Christian should of course inspire the most tolerance." Then he added, "but until now Christians have been the most intolerant of all men." I might accuse Voltaire of having a jaundiced view of Christianity, but one of the 20th century's most beloved Bible teachers, Dr. J. Vernon McGee, said, "There's nothing meaner than a Christian when he is mean."

Christians are even judgmental against each other. A Christian speaker, Joyce Meyer, once asked the disturbing question, "Do you know how many people come to church mad?" Then she added the even more disturbing observation, "And half the time they are coming to church with the people they're mad at."

Judgment is an effective tool for separating myself from another. Any temptation to look with disdain or contempt upon another—even when I don't say anything—kills the possibility of true compassion. To the extent that religion provides a base for cutting myself off from others, I am not going to be religious.

A priest named Father Ron said to a group of people, "What will save us in the end is not what we said or thought but how we lived with each other." I was moved by his words. Father Ron's comment wouldn't have made such an impact upon me except that he spoke them during the rededication of an Islamic Center after it had been rebuilt following a horrible fire that was set by anti-Muslim terrorists.

True religion consists of getting into close relationship with God and, by the same faith-prompted movement, getting into relationship with the people around me, as well—holding "God and man in one thought at one time, at all times." Entering into full-hearted relationship with God and with all the people in my life unlocks resources of power and freedom within my own heart. The Bible is full of texts about the power of unreciprocated love—not as sectarian teachings, but as spiritual truths that any wise person can discover by personal experience. Buddha said, "In the end these things matter most: How well did you love? How fully did you love? How deeply did you learn to let go?"

We speak about unconditional love, but sometimes offer mere lip service. I am in the process of loving people with neither caveat nor reservation; engaging with God above and the people around me with all my heart.

# Try This

1.  *Identify some dogma or teaching that you've used as a basis for disregarding others or treating them with contempt.*

2.  *Do something thoughtful to one of those people today; let an act of kindness mitigate your harsh belief.*

# Day 52—Reflect Deeply Upon Life

*There is one art of which man should be master, the art of reflection. –Samuel Taylor Coleridge*

Life is beautiful when I engage with important issues by deep reflection leading to new understandings. At that point life becomes like a dance, moving me with grace through the various steps.

Coleridge's comment in this instruction's key quote echoes Socrates' much more famous observation that "The unexamined life is not worth living." We might infer from the two similar quotes that past societies, as well, were populated by those who maintained the lethargic mentality marking couch potato-people in our contemporary culture. I am only able to put my whole self into life by avoiding any temptation to live according to tired principles and rules that my teachers, parents, or acquaintances handed to me. I grow and thrive through processes of experience and learning that challenge my belief system and even confront the basic principles by which I live. I have great respect for the declaration by Reverend Jerry Hanoum: "I don't care how troublesome the truth may be; I just want to know the truth."

Of course, "truth" can sometimes have a slippery quality because any fearlessly objective approach to the subject continually involves the seeker in contradictions and paradoxes. Reflection can sometimes be an uncomfortable exercise, because unshakable certainty only becomes possible by pretending some things to be absolutely true while shutting myself off from other apparently contradictory true things.

The one unquestionable truth by which I order my life is the fact that the universe is under control of benevolent forces that continually move me towards the light, if I am only in the place of being movable. I preserve that movability by practicing the art of reflection that Coleridge referred to. I take time, for example, to reflect upon the reason for any confusing behavior that I had participated in that day. I also make an effort to be alone with my thoughts and meditate upon the meaning of some amazing hypothesis that I might have encountered.

My greatest conceptual breakthroughs come in response to pain; my greatest insights result from sorrow or even tragedy. I grow as I embrace difficult experiences with both arms, not trying to avoid uncomfortable feelings. I learned things about healthy attitudes through my bout with cancer that I could never have learned otherwise. I learned lessons about the comfort of God through the death of my brother-in-law Rodney that I would never have learned in any other way.

Change and growth come through reflection as Hegelian-like motions of synthesizing incompatible propositions. For example, the thesis that "I am healthy and well" encounters the awful antithesis that "I have got cancer" leading to the synthesis, "My cancer can't harm my wellbeing at this moment. Right now I am still okay."

The powerful thing about this kind of reflective process in the face of the most terrible events is that negative stressful experiences possess a potential to raise me to a subsequent level of living that is deeper and richer than the comfortable position I started from. The power of reflection can use negative experiences as the means of increasing my wisdom.

Joni Mitchell's lyrical song, "Both Sides Now," captures the movements that I am talking about. She sings of how her attitudes towards clouds, love, and life went from fairy tale like illusions, to a disillusioned state, to a final state in which she realized that those things were greater than she could comprehend or define.

# Try This

1. *Think about the last argument you had over some point of belief or conviction. Move yourself into an ego-state in which you are willing to consider that perhaps you were wrong, or at least that you might have more to learn about the point you were arguing for.*

2. *Answer the question, "My life goal is_____."  Carefully consider whether this is the best goal for you to have, or whether another might make you better for yourself, for others, and for heaven's sake.*

## Day 53—Get Rid of Old Nonsense

*Finish each day and be done with it. You have done what you could. Some blunders and absurdities no doubt crept in; forget them as soon as you can. Tomorrow is a new day; begin it well and serenely and with too high a spirit to be cumbered with your old nonsense –Ralph Waldo Emerson*

My ability to seriously engage in life on a healthy and productive level requires the experience Emerson describes in the key quote of each day putting behind me the mistakes and failures of the previous day.

What is missing from Emerson's advice is any hint of how I can ever manage successfully to do that. It is easy enough to say the words about my failings, "forget them as soon as you can." However, what if I can't forget them in any amount of time? Or, worse, what if my "forgetting" of them means that I simply shove them into some space in my unconscious mind where they fester and eventually erupt in some outpouring of incomprehensible psychic darkness? Some of us are carrying around burdens of shame for "old nonsense' and regretting "blunders and absurdities" that we committed years ago. In some cases, decades.

Malicious comments made by parents, siblings, children, relatives, schoolmates, fellow workers, and neighbors—or even strangers—can burn into our spirits, and demolish the possibility of beginning any day "well and serenely." The words and behaviors of politicians and celebrities can arouse in our hearts deep feelings of resentment and even hatred that pollute our tranquility and deny to us the *joie de vivre* that should be our birthright as human beings fashioned by a Benevolent Creator to enjoy the pleasures of His creation.

Every day I must rediscover sources of forgiveness and grace that will make it possible for me to move beyond the blunders and absurdities committed by others and especially by myself. I must learn honestly to admit my failures, inadequacies, and resentments—admitting them first to myself and then before Heaven—seeking the sense of forgiveness and release that will make it possible for me to "forget them," as Emerson says I must.

That act of receiving forgiveness provides a basis from which I can then forgive everyone else for whatever they've done to harm me—whether or not they deserve my forgiveness. It is possible, perhaps even necessary, for me to engage in forgiveness as a fundamentally selfish act—forgiving people because I desperately need to free myself from the acids of resentment that will otherwise burn into my soul. And I do!

I deliberately pray every day, confessing my failures, determining not to repeat them, and then receiving the sense of forgiveness that Heaven continually offers to me. Only at that point can I then quickly put away any anger or resentment that I might have against anybody else in the world. Processes of forgiveness and restoration create an environment for the "high spirits" that Emerson wrote about. "You turned my wailing into dancing," sang the Psalmist. "You removed my sackcloth and clothed me with joy."

The universe contains ugly and awful things, for sure, but these days I am absolutely enveloped in a world that is permeated by the possibilities for doing good and receiving good from others. A wonderful bonus grows out of this daily experience: The process of confession, repentance, and forgiveness empowers me to deny permission to old habits that pull me down; to not keep repeating day-after-day tiresome and depressing patterns of personal failure and resentment.

I really am "getting rid of my old nonsense." My life is an upward spiral—each day seemingly more joyful and fuller of the power for daily living than the day before.

# Try This

1.  *Right now, pray for the power of Heaven to cleanse your mind and will from those "blunders and absurdities" that are pulling you down.*

2.  *Based on that cleansing, begin to live "well and serenely and with too high a spirit to be cumbered with your old nonsense."*

# Day 54—Dance with Your Eyes Wide Open

*Science without religion is lame, religion without science is blind.* —*Albert Einstein*

Becoming fully engaged in all material, social, and spiritual aspects of the universe requires that I be neither lame nor blind, to use the words of Einstein from the key quote for this instruction. Confusion of boundaries between science and religion—especially concerning origins—continually generates unnecessary friction in this world and prevents me from enjoying the proper fruits belonging to each.

Mistaken approaches towards evolutionism and creationism have worked together to create a matched set of equal and opposite errors because Evolutionism attempts to elevate a scientific theory into a religion or philosophy, while Creationism seeks to diminish theological doctrine to mere scientific theory. Both sides confuse the subject that they claim to explain.

Scientists (or lay people, for that matter) are certainly confused when they say things like, "There is no God because the universe simply came about through evolutionary processes." Such science-based assertions about the absence of God are based upon fuzzy thinking; no theory of origins could possibly answer such philosophical questions as, "By what power and for what purpose, if any, did the world come into being?" Any assertion that the scientific method could be used to discover Ultimate Truth stems from bad science leading to worse philosophy. The only reasonable and ethical purely scientific response to philosophical questions about the existence of a Creator or purpose for existence is to say, "Nothing in science provides answers."

Scientists of course share with the rest of us the frailties associated with the human race, so some scientists are neither reasonable nor ethical. A few of them attempt to employ their pseudo-philosophical doctrine of Evolutionism as a weapon against a religious worldview.

Some religious people commit the opposite kind of error from that committed by doctrinaire scientific atheists. Just as evolutionists suppose the findings of science to have *philosophical* legitimacy, some religious people suppose the language of the Bible (or of the Hindu Upanishads, for that matter) carry *scientific* validity. For students of religion to suppose they can form a scientific theory based upon religious writings is just as wrong as scientists supposing they can use the scientific method to derive theological dogma.

Biblical literalists are just as wrong to imagine that God meant the language of the seven days of creation to be taken in support of some Young Earth theory as they formerly were wrong when they used the biblical language about the sun riding from one side of the earth to the other (Psalm 19:4-6) in support of the Geocentric theory—that the earth is the center of the universe.

The only reasonable and ethical response of religious scholars to the cosmological question of origins is to say, "Nothing in religion can provide answers." The creation passage obviously asserts that the Spirit of God is behind the physical world that we see—reflecting in part at least the Upanishads' teaching that birth and death of humans on earth or of galaxies in outer space are the changing manifestations of God.

I am grateful for the promises of the Bible that illuminate my daily life—glad to live in a universe full of purpose and order. I am also thankful for the advances of science and have always been fascinated by the power of the microscope and telescope to reveal things about the universe that God continues to create.

Neither lame nor blind, I wish to dance through this world amazed by the miraculous things I see around me, beneath my feet, and above my head. I want to live my life in perfect harmony with the One who inhabits them all.

And by His grace, I do!

# Try This

1.  *This week read Psalm 104 and give thanks that you are part of a great scheme that has been moving forward from the foundation of the world.*

2.  *Read a scientific book or at least an article about the universe.*

# Day 55—Embrace Life as it Is

*We should manage our fortunes as we do our health—enjoy it when good, be patient when it is bad, and never apply violent remedies except in an extreme necessity.*
*–Francois de La Rochefoucauld*

A necessary part of any full engagement in life has been for me to learn to accept whatever life sends my way—accepting the bad along with the good, and submitting myself to the reality that from my limited viewpoint I can't tell what is ultimately good or bad nor discern whether any particular event is, in fact, helpful or harmful.

A poor woodcutter came across a beautiful white horse that had been lost in the woods. When he brought the horse to his village, the villagers exclaimed how beautiful the animal was and how fortunate the man had been to find it. The man's son learned to ride the horse but one day the horse threw him to the ground, he broke his leg, and after that always walked with a limp. The villagers then exclaimed how unfortunate it was, after all, that the woodcutter had been to find the horse. Otherwise, his son would not have been injured.

Not long after that, a group of soldiers came riding into the little village and drafted into the military all the young men in the village except for the lame son of the poor woodcutter. Once again, the foolish villagers exclaimed how fortunate the discovery of the beautiful horse had turned out to be after all. Otherwise, his son would not have been injured and would have been taken off to war with the other young men.

Awful things that happen to people often turn out to be blessings in disguise. A man in Scotland reportedly scrimped and saved for years in order to move himself, his wife, and his nine children to America. As the departure day approached, they had their belongings packed and their passports ready. The dream was shattered only a week before the boat was scheduled to sail when a dog bit the youngest son. The doctor bandaged the wound but then placed the boy under a mandatory two-week quarantine.

The father's heart was filled with rage and disappointment as he stood on the dock and watched the beautiful ship sail for America leaving him and his family behind. The father was angry with God for allowing this to happen and enraged at his son for being bitten by the dog. However, a few days later the headlines were filled with the news that the ship they were to sail on—the Titanic—had sunk beneath the waves taking hundreds of passengers to a watery grave. When the father learned of the tragedy he embraced his son and gave thanks to God for keeping his family alive. What had seemed to be a curse had actually turned into a blessing.

I have learned to embrace life as it comes to me and to avoid the feelings of bitterness, anger, and disappointment that come from life not living up to the artificial expectations that I had for it. Uncomfortable things that come into my life all have a constructive effect when I face them with optimism and courage. "Man needs difficulties," Carl Jung declared. Then he added, "They are necessary for health." When I contracted cancer I became aware of resources of grace that I had never discovered before; I developed a capacity to reach out to others that I had not previously possessed.

I no longer pray fervently that God will protect me from disease, poverty, or some other catastrophe. His Presence is with me to face whatever comes along and to completely embrace life however it comes to me. I find such steady composure to be more satisfying than health; more comforting than fame; more gratifying than wealth.

# Try This

1. *Consider 2-3 unanticipated positive outcomes from the last great disappointment that you experienced.*

2. *The next time life seems to be letting you down, actively search for some advantage, resource, or blessing that you might otherwise have missed.*

# Day 56—Don't Bother Preparing for Death

*He who does not prepare for death is more than an ordinary
fool, he is a madman. –Spurgeon*

It would be a common sort of wisdom to say that nobody could put
his/her whole self into life without first being prepared to die, but my own
experience reverses that because acts of engaging completely with life, by
themselves, seem to provide sufficient preparation for death. This was surely
what Leonardo da Vinci was thinking when he noted that, "As a well spent
day brings happy sleep, so life well used brings happy death." A person whose
life is awash in grace prepares to die by being thoroughly involved in living.

A story is told about Francis of Assisi that while he was hoeing his
garden one day, someone asked him, "What would you do if you suddenly
learned that you were to die at sunset today?" Saint Francis replied, "I would
finish hoeing my garden."

Beyond the obvious task of making a will, it's difficult for me to think
about actually preparing for death, as Spurgeon insists in this instruction's key
quote that I prepare for it. I have a current will. I can't think of any other thing
I need to do. Elizabeth Kübler-Ross defined five stages in the process of dying
that, she says, people normally go through:

1. Denial and Isolation
2. Anger
3. Bargaining
4. Depression, and
5. Acceptance.

I am probably as ready to die as any man can be without actually having
some terminal illness. Perhaps the approach of my final hour will trouble
my mind and spirit because I was certainly shocked a few years ago when
diagnosed with cancer. I am prepared to have some difficulty making the
Final Transition, but I think that I am mostly finished with the process.

Death is just one part of the experience of life. In fact, Kübler-Ross
wrote a book called *Death: The Final Stage of Growth*. My life is buoyed up by
an incredible sense of being held by strong arms; guided by a brilliant light;
swept along in a shining river. I am sure that the arms are eternal, the light is
shining from Heaven, and the river's mouth is Eternity.

# How to Put Your Whole Self In

An obvious corollary to my attitude is the belief that every event in my life is part of a sequence leading to a wonderful conclusion. This being the case, it makes absolutely no sense for me to do anything except to express thanksgiving and praise no matter what comes into my life. "We rejoice in our sufferings," the Bible says (Romans 5:3). Not because we derive masochistic pleasure from our pain, but because we know that a loving God wouldn't permit any dark thing in our life unless some good would come out of it. The great Christian writer Oswald Chambers noted:

> It is only a faithful person who truly believes that God sovereignly controls his circumstances. We take our circumstances for granted, saying God is in control, but not really believing it. We act as if the things that happen were completely controlled by people.

The blessed life of grace I live today has an eternal dimension. Someday I will die. I fully expect the actual, literal experience in that mysterious other dimension to be far more wonderful than the current, earthly experiences of my life.

The last stage in dying, according to Elizabeth Kübler-Ross's research, is Acceptance. I think I have skipped the other four steps. All that stuff about denial, and anger, and trying to negotiate with God.... What would be the point of it for me? I am living life one day at a time, which is just the way I expect to live my last day.

# Try This

1. *Before you do anything else, give your life with all your hopes, fears, ambitions, conflicts, jealousy, and anger to God, however you understand Him to be.*

2. *As part of your preparation for death, take some deliberate action that will bless your life and/or that will encourage or assist someone else.*

DR. DONALD HUNTINGTON

## Day 57—Understand That You Don't Understand Much

*Opinion has caused more trouble on this little earth than plagues or earthquakes. —Voltaire*

One of the great insights that makes full engagement with life easier—or even possible, perhaps—is my full-hearted acceptance of the fact that I can't discern the ultimate meaning and purpose of the complex matrix of existence that I am caught up in.

I sometimes wonder if the existence of high school debate teams doesn't bring into question the validity of all views of reality. Two opposing sides, each taking arbitrary and opposing viewpoints on a controversial subject, are convincingly able to marshal facts and evidence in support of whichever side they find themselves on. The processes of research and argumentation often drive debaters eventually to believe strongly in whichever viewpoint they have been assigned to support. This truth about debate teams has bothered me for years. I realize that under the right circumstances (or wrong circumstances) I could probably convince myself of the truth of almost any position. I have firm convictions about a number of things, but no longer have supreme confidence that I actually understand those issues correctly or completely.

I have been able completely to flip-flop my thoughts on one subject or another far too often for comfort. Something that seemed obviously true yesterday, and for which I was able to present what seemed to me compelling arguments, appears today to be false. I am able now to present what seems to me compelling arguments for exactly the opposite position than I previously held on some issues.

One of the greatest Christian writers, G.K. Chesterton, spoke the truth when he said that it is not bigotry to be certain we are right but that it is bigotry to be unable to imagine how we might possibly have gone wrong. By Chesterton's standard I am no bigot. I am certain of some things, but I most certainly know exactly how I might have gone wrong in coming to my certainties.

Perhaps I have changed my opinions too often but the famous French Renaissance writer, Michel de Montaigne, believed that "Stubborn and ardent clinging to one's opinion is the best proof of stupidity." Bertrand Russell chimed in on this point with a sage observation: "A big problem in this world is that the idiots are convinced that they know everything and the intelligent people are full of doubts." He's probably right because the fact is that I have never met one fool who entertained the slightest degree of uncertainty about his/her opinions.

I am trying to be more humble these days about stating my beliefs, no matter how certain my reasoning seems to be. Also, I am trying to focus more on relationships—approaching God as a You, rather than as a He while striving to serve, respect, and even to admire the people around me. These acts and attitudes seem to be beyond reason; they are the cornerstone—the fundamental basis upon which my philosophy of life and service finds direction and perspective.

I am grateful that I don't have to have an opinion on everything in the world! No matter how bewildering it is, life affords me plenty of opportunities to serve God and to love others! The effort of trying to rise to those opportunities always makes perfect sense to me and is enough to fill my life with meaning.

If only I have the will to put my whole self into life, it seems to me that I have crystal clarity concerning the truth about the attitudes and tasks demanded of me right now. That's enough truth!

# Try This

1. *Think about any pointless argument you might have had in the recent past. Did anyone profit from the arguing? Did you accomplish anything by maintaining your opinion?*

2. *Make up your mind to prevent opinions from ever harming your loving relationship with anyone in your life.*

# Day 58—Question Everything

*In all affairs it's a healthy thing now and then to hang a*
*question mark on the things you have long taken for granted.*
*—Bertrand Russell*

One of the important qualities that make it possible for me to put my whole self into relationships and tasks lies in a continual reassessment of my viewpoint of life and of my understanding of what is true. I question everything. I willingly comply with Thomas Jefferson's ringing admonition:

> *Shake off all the fears of servile prejudices, under which weak*
> *minds are servilely crouched. Fix reason firmly in her seat, and*
> *call on her tribunal for every fact, every opinion. Question*
> *with boldness even the existence of a God; because, if there be*
> *one, he must more approve of the homage of reason than that*
> *of blindfolded fear.*

Marilyn vos Savant, who is listed in the *Guinness Book of World Records* Hall of Fame as having the highest recorded IQ (228), once made a comment that appealed to my uncertainty about even fundamental beliefs: "I question myself more than anyone I know," she wrote. "Some might consider this a weakness, but I believe it is one of my greatest strengths."

The English historian and Renaissance scholar, Bishop Mandell Creighton, posed an observation that was as thoughtful as it was surprising (given his rank and position): "The one real object of education is to have a man in the condition of continually asking questions." As Voltaire noted, "Doubt is not a pleasant mental state but certainty is a ridiculous one."

I find it reassuring that these brilliant people acknowledge the importance of questioning life, since I also feel compelled continually to evaluate my positions and continually to "tweak" my worldview. If I am rationalizing my position, at least my rationalizations have deliberate and ongoing connections with my actual experiences. The fact is that, as Gordon Atkinson, who writes under the pseudonym "Real Live Preacher," noted, "Fidelity to commitment in the face of doubts and fears is a very spiritual thing." Then he went on to note, "People who doubt can have great faith because faith is something you do, not something you think." And then Atkinson added a final punch line, "In fact, the greater your doubt the more heroic your faith."

Even though I could doubt even the ultimate goodness of the universe as created and sustained by a benevolent God, I am continually reassured by my realization that, though the world is full of suffering, it is also filled with examples about the overcoming of it, as Helen Keller reminded us. There is plenty in the world around me to continually confirm my belief that the universe is ultimately benevolent. I have discovered the world to be full of grace by personal experience; a Presence is with me to guide me; a Divine Companion who loves me and who fills my heart with love for others. I don't just "feel" this to be true. I question it all the time, but the response is one of continual validation.

I am on a pilgrimage to an amazing destination. I am daily learning by experience the truth the Bible speaks of:

> *His divine power has given us everything we need for life and godliness through our knowledge of him who called us by his own glory and goodness. Through these he has given us his very great and precious promises, so that through them you may participate in the divine nature and escape the corruption in the world caused by evil desires (2 Peter 1:3-4).*

Those "very great and precious promises" continually become demonstrably true in my life. The Master turns every question mark I hang on those promises into an exclamation mark of His reassuring presence.

# Try This

1. *Consider some of your core beliefs that might be preventing you from engaging completely in life and may be hindering your relationship with the people around you.*

2. *Make up your mind to examine your thinking about those things, even if it means that you may surrender some long-held and cherished opinion.*

# Day 59—Commit to Life-Long Learning

*I don't divide the world into the weak and the strong, or the successes and the failures, those who make it or those who don't. I divide the world into learners and non-learners.*
*–Benjamin Barber*

Nobody who is confident about their grasp of what's going on in the world or satisfied with the quality of their own knowledge and wisdom can fully engage in life or put their whole self into relationships with other people.

I am sometimes overwhelmed by the extent of my lack of knowledge. The fact is that I am in good company in feeling completely humbled by my ignorance. Plato referred to Socrates as "an idol, a master figure…, a Saint," and "a prophet." About himself, Socrates reportedly made the comment, "The Delphic oracle said I was the wisest of all the Greeks." However, he then added, "It is because I alone, of all the Greeks, know that I know nothing."

I am in a lifelong process of becoming constantly more aware of the limitations of my knowledge. My attitude about limited knowledge is nothing more than frank acknowledgement of the incomprehensible nature of the world about me—both in its physical and in its spiritual manifestations. The fact is that the awareness of my limitations is the beginning of wisdom because for a long time what I thought I knew prevented me from learning anything new. Whenever I meet anyone who thinks they know a lot, I realize that they really do have a lot to learn. Because I can't learn everything, I must choose the things I will master, which necessarily involves letting go of others. Making that choice wisely is one of the most important tasks I face in this life.

Coming to true wisdom requires more than head knowledge. The wisdom that really informs my life and changes me always results from praxis, which is the process that embodies theories, doctrines, skills, and principles in the real world through application, testing, and confirmation. Aristotle defined praxis as the practical operation of wisdom and knowledge to a final goal of some sort of action. Only by such practical application can knowledge be driven into my heart and be converted into wisdom that will transform my choices and behaviors.

# How to Put Your Whole Self In

Sometimes I think it is crazy how little I really learn about the Master's ways and how poorly I actually practice His presence. However, Ann Lamott wrote words that speak to my heart:

> *Big is the magic we look for first, but grace is what makes things work out against all odds. If it were too big, it might sweep away all the bits of knowledge and insight we're granted as we go along. If it were too big, it couldn't get through the almost invisible cracks and holes in our walls, in our stone hearts; knowledge comes in tendrils.*

I am so thankful for Lamott's words. In my heart I know that she speaks the truth. The knowledge of the truth seeps slowly but steadily into my spirit. The "tendrils" of His ways are slowly poking into all the parts of my life. I am a slow learner, but I will never stop trying better to learn His ways with me.

My willingness to learn and the constant acts of doing so are essential parts of the process of putting my whole self into life. Coming to a state of smug satisfaction with my knowledge and wisdom would make me a useless person indeed.

# Try This

1. *Think about the last new thing you learned and about the manner in which you learned it.*

2. *Go to Wikipedia.com and find one thing you never knew before. Take some action to apply the knowledge to your life.*

# Day 60—Listen Meaning into Silence

*The most important thing in communication is to hear what isn't being said. –Peter Drucker*

People who put their whole selves into life and into relationships with others inevitably come to discover the power of stillness; they learn that some of the most amazing acts of communication are conveyed through nothing more than profound silence.

The wife of President Calvin Coolidge once commissioned a portrait for her husband. The president walked into the library accompanied by a senator and the two of them stared at the picture together in silence. Coolidge finally commented quietly: "I think so too."

Silence can be a powerful medium for communication. I read a moving account of a small boy who went to visit an elderly neighbor who had recently lost his wife to death. When the child returned his mom asked him what he said to the neighbor. "I didn't say anything to him," the boy replied. "I just sat on his lap and helped him cry." Saying anything would have diminished the effectiveness of his communication.

A pastor told me that he once received a chilling call informing him that an elder in his church had just killed a child by backing his truck over him. "What are you going to say to him?" his wife asked the pastor, as he was getting ready to leave.

"If I have to say anything to him then I am not going!" he answered.

We comfort each other in times of distress by our hugs and tears—not by words nor by any attempted explanations about the situation. Acknowledgement of the power of silence lies behind Dave Tyson Gentry's observation that "True friendship comes when silence between two people is comfortable."

Silence and repose provide refuge for my spirit from the storms of my life. Communicating with Heaven has analogies with communicating with anyone. In a sense God speaks to me through the Bible—telling me what He desires from me, setting the conditions for my continuing in relationship with Him, and especially giving me the promises that form the basis for my life of grace.

On another equally important level however, God communicates by not saying anything; He communicates by silence. "Be still, and know that I am God," He says. Until I really do that—until I listen to the silence that surrounds Him and listen to what isn't being said—I can't experience the full blessing of God's presence.

Prayer is the other side of that communication. When my heart is just too full for verbal communication the communication of my silence will always be wonderfully effective. The Bible says that, when I am beyond the capacity for oral utterance, the Spirit of God will help me in my "weakness."

Heaven enters my soul and speaks His silent message into my heart every day. I am learning to listen. My soul resonates in harmony with ee comings' wonderful words:

> *I am a little church*
> *–far from the frantic*
> *world with its rapture and anguish at peace with nature*
> *–I do not worry if longer nights grow longest;*
>
> *I am not sorry when silence becomes singing*

I am slowly becoming better at allowing God to sing into the silence of my spirit; and have learned sometimes to listen myself into the silence that surrounds Him; when I am at my best, circumstances are able to make a song of my silence.

# Try This

1. *The next time you speak with a spouse, family member, or close friend tune yourself to body movement, pauses, and facial expressions to listen to what the person is communicating beyond speech.*

2. *Look for opportunities to use silence as a means of consoling or comforting someone going through a difficult experience.*

# Day 61—Expect Miracles

*There are only two ways to live your life. One is as though nothing is a miracle. The other is as though everything is a miracle. —Albert Einstein*

I suspected for a long time that people who said things like "everything is a miracle," as Einstein does in the key quote, are merely using a subterfuge for expressing their core disbelief that God actually intervenes in our world from outside our normal space/time continuum.

The world is full of people who deny the possibility of miraculous phenomena. However, nobody can deny the reality of miracles, on one hand, without entertaining an unquestioning faith that miracles are impossible on the other. C.S. Lewis pointed out the circular argument necessarily involved in any philosophical position against miracles:

*We know the experience against miracles to be uniform only if we know that all reports of them are false. And we can know all the reports to be false only if we know already that miracles have never occurred. In fact, we are arguing in a circle.*

The more experiences I have the more I begin to regard my life as being a matrix of miracles, as Einstein apparently believed. Powerful forces from beyond our mundane world are continually influencing the course of our lives. The mother of a seriously disabled child wrote the insightful words,

*I thought I would have to teach my son about the world, turns out I have to teach the world about my son. They see a boy who doesn't speak, I see a miracle who doesn't need words.*

*—Jayna Sattler*

A power for good is continually intervening in the world in special ways. I see God's hand in the lives of my family, through the affection of my friends, in the faces of the people I worship with, in the events taking place in my professional life.... The life of devotion that I currently am living has powerfully opened my eyes—not merely to discerning God's gracious interventions on my behalf, but seeing Him also work in me, as well, and occasionally even through me. I am surrounded by miracles.

# How to Put Your Whole Self In

My experience is not unique. The world is full of people who, like Einstein, regard the world as being full of miracles. A noted ornithologist, Hugh Elliott, wrote the stirring words:

> *Miracles: You do not have to look for them. They are there, 24/7, beaming like radio waves all around you. Put up the antenna, turn up the volume—snap... crackle... this just in, every person you talk to is a chance to change the world....*

My life is less religious these days than ever before. Daily realities sweep away the importance of the words I use to express the things that are happening to me. Part of the reason for the experience I am having with my miraculous life comes from acts of deliberately putting my whole self into life. "When we do the best that we can," Helen Keller said, "we never know what miracle is wrought in our life, or in the life of another."

I have been breaking down the wall separating the spiritual side of my life from my secular activities. The Bible observes that "...we know that in all things God works for the good of those who love him, who have been called according to his purpose" (Romans 8:28). In other words, God is working "in all things" in my life to bring me to a place He has planned for me.

I have never been more convinced than I am now that this "work" is always going on and, by hindsight, has been going for years. Reality dazzles me every day. Everything is a miracle!

# Try This

1. *Reflect upon one time in your life when something occurred that you felt in your heart couldn't possibly have happened because of luck or mere coincidence.*

2. *Expect that today miracles of guidance and encouragement will take place in your life. Look for them. They surround you.*

# Day 62—Embrace the Surprising Joy of Humility

*If anyone would like to acquire humility ... the first step is
to realize that one is proud ... nothing whatever can be done
before it. If you think you are not conceited, it means you are
very conceited indeed.* —C.S. Lewis

I know by personal experience that C.S. Lewis is right about the humble person not feeling humble. Any feelings I might have of humility—any personal experiences of satisfaction from thinking that I am not conceited—become themselves signs of conceit, as C.S. Lewis' quote points out.

Rick Warren—author of *The Purpose Driven Life*—hit a nail right on the head when he wrote, "Humility is not thinking less of yourself; it is thinking of yourself less." He is exactly right because pride and conceit always turn to manipulation and self-gratification; true humility turns upward towards serving Heaven and outward towards serving our fellow human beings.

The conceited person may imagine such things as, "I am a good person," but the truly humble person will be focusing on thoughts like, "What does the Universe want from me today?" or "What is the best thing I can do for that particular person?"

I may perform many acts either for selfish or for humble reasons. For example, I may give an automobile to my daughter as a means of binding her more tightly to my parental authority. On the other hand, I may give it to her in order to permit her to more freely pursue her own goals and purposes. In the first case, I am acting selfishly, even though I might congratulate myself on being an apparently loving person. In the second case, I am acting in true humility and generosity. I won't be inclined to think anything about what the act shows about me as a person, but will only be grateful to be a source of aid and blessing for my daughter.

Perhaps a test for discerning the difference between humility and vanity lies in figuring out how good I feel about any praise or gratitude that follows my performing an act of kindness. As a proud person, I will always insist upon enthusiastic displays of gratitude for anything I do for another person. In humility, on the other hand, I will neither look for, nor even notice particularly, if the person is grateful or not because of the joy that comes from being able to contribute to the happiness of someone I love. The purity of my motives becomes suspect when I am too pleased by my daughter's gratitude for her new car or too offended by any ingratitude.

A natural tendency by good people is to "settle the score"—to attempt to repay us for whatever we give. The best kind of service, therefore, will be anonymous. The next best way to maintain a spirit of humility while preserving another person's sense of worth is to tell them not to pay us back for anything we do but to pay it forward—helping someone else as we might have helped them. In this way we become change agents by creating dynamic processes of small improvements in "this place of wrath and tears." The world grows sweeter and more pleasant by multiplied small selfless acts of kindness; by innumerable and unnoticed deeds of mercy.

Humility brings me to a healthy place where I can become a whole person. Only through joy-filled selflessness can my eyes be open to the miracles that flow about me. As Thoreau observed, "Humility like darkness reveals the heavenly lights." This is so remarkable! The brightness and good cheer of genuine humility is surely one of the most astonishing facts in this dark world!

# Try This

1.   *Find one person today that you can do something nice for without them knowing who you are, if possible.*

2.   *Reflect upon how much more satisfying the generous act was than if you demanded or even hoped for some show of gratitude.*

# Day 63—Be Small Enough Each Night to go to Bed

*Humility is perfect quietness of heart. It is for me to have no trouble; never to be fretted or vexed or irritated or sore or disappointed. It is to expect nothing, to wonder at nothing that is done to me, to feel nothing done against me. It is to be at rest when nobody praises me and when I am blamed or despised.....*
*–Andrew Murray*

My mother was a woman of good humor but was not a humorist. During her 92 years, as far as I can remember, she only told one joke. She said that when she was young she got a special ribbon for being the most humble person in Sunday school. They took the ribbon away from her the very next week because she wore it.

A scientist named William Beebe reported a memorable story about Teddy Roosevelt. He and the president would sometimes have dinner together. During fine weather at the conclusion of their evenings, Beebe said that he and the president would sometimes take a walk on the White House lawn. Roosevelt would scan the skies for a certain spot. When he found it, he would point to it and say:

*That is the Spiral Galaxy in Andromeda. It is as large as our Milky Way. It is one of a hundred million galaxies. It consists of one hundred billion suns, each larger than our sun.*

Then the president of the United States would say, "Now I think we are small enough! Let's go to bed."

The Bible says, "Do not think of yourself more highly than you ought, but rather think of yourself with sober judgment, in accordance with the measure of faith God has given you" (Romans 12:3). C.S. Lewis made this perceptive observation:

*Do not imagine that if you meet a really humble man he will be what most people call "humble" nowadays: he will not be a sort of greasy, smarmy person, who is always telling you that, of course, he is nobody. Probably all you will think about him is that he seemed a cheerful, intelligent chap who took a real*

*interest in what you said to him.... He will not be thinking
about humility: he will not be thinking about himself at all.*
*–C. S. Lewis*

One mark of truly humble people is that they lack the ability to look down on others except for those times in which they are engaged in helping fallen people get to their feet. People who are full of themselves, on the other hand, often display a sense of self-satisfaction or complacency, but none of them are ever truly happy, because their lives are necessarily shallow. They are too thrilled by the imagined brilliance of their own efforts and ideas to catch the smallest glimpse of the rich lives of the people who surround them. Their worlds orbit around their own feelings and accomplishments so they can never step back and marvel at the works of God or the accomplishments of another person. They are unable ever to come to the place where they are "small enough to go to bed."

Thoreau once made the important observation, "Humility like darkness reveals the heavenly lights." I want to be like President Roosevelt when I come to retire in the evening. Even when night falls on the final day of my life, I hope I won't lie down until I am small enough to realize once again the wonders of creation—and the even more marvelous wonders of the ways of God's grace in this world. At that moment I expect my eyes to be open to gaze upon even greater wonders and my mind open to comprehend mysteries that for now remain inscrutable to the most humble imagination.

# Try This

1. *Spend a little time each day considering the vastness of the
   universe as seen both in the starry firmament and in the
   incomprehensible complexities of a single flower or blade
   of grass.*

2. *Permit yourself to be properly humbled as you find your
   own role as a part of that immensity and sharing in
   that complexity.*

# Day 64—Don't Forgive Until You're Ready

*It is never too late to forgive. But you can forgive too soon.*
*I am especially wary of what I call "saintly forgiveness."*
*Premature forgiveness is common among people who avoid*
*conflict. They're afraid of their own anger and the anger*
*of others. But their forgiveness is false. Their anger goes*
*underground. —Robert Karen*

There is a danger in attempting to be moral and upright through an outside-in imposition of rules of behavior rather than as an inside-out process of character development. When someone has wronged me the appropriate course of action is to forgive the individual from my heart—if for no other reason than to maintain the sense of joy, serenity, and peace of mind that I ought to expect and even demand from life. Beyond that, of course, is the less selfish motivations of giving to the offending individual the same consideration that I hope and long for from people whom I have myself wronged in some way.

However, as this instruction's key quote points out, if I do harbor burning resentment in my heart against another person, the absolutely wrong course of action is for me to pretend that those feelings are not there. The world's most famous proponent of peace, Gandhi, recognized the difference between genuine peace and mere compliance. "It is better to be violent," he wrote, "if there is violence in our hearts, than to put on the cloak of nonviolence to cover impotence."

The "impotence" Gandhi spoke about plays a key role in getting straight the matter of forgiveness because in another place he made the accurate observation: "The weak can never forgive. Forgiveness is the attribute of the strong." That being the case, I must strengthen myself in order to reach the point at which I am strong enough to forgive people for whatever harm they may have done to me. Such strength can come about through mental and spiritual exercises such as purposeful reading and deliberate reflection that strengthen my spirit—analogous to physical exercises that strengthen my body.

Control over my thought-life is the fundamental means of developing strength sufficient to forgive people from my heart for any injury. I grow in strength by following a biblical admonition "….whatever is true, whatever is noble, whatever is right, whatever is pure, whatever is lovely, whatever is admirable—if anything is excellent or praiseworthy—think about such things" (Philippians 4:8).

Of course, forgiveness is not appropriate in some circumstances. The fact that Gandhi was a man of peace did not mean that he overlooked the fact that evil people were doing awful things. Even at that point, however, Gandhi did much more than merely brood and harbor bitter feelings in his heart. He learned to channel his wrath into productive responses in the service of justice. Gandhi wrote,

> I have learned through bitter experience the one supreme lesson
> to conserve my anger, and as heat conserved is transmitted into
> energy, even so our anger controlled can be transmitted into a
> power that can move the world.

The purest form of anger—and the one least harmful to myself—is anger that is expressed on behalf of injustice shown to someone else. In the case of child abuse, for example, my appropriate response is to make whatever intervention is possible on behalf of the abused child. At the point of the abuse the time has not yet arrived for forgiving the abusive person. I must also confront acts of overt racism or sexism with righteous anger by interceding on behalf of the offended individual but always with the ultimate intention of moving finally towards peace, forgiveness, and reconciliation if such outcomes are at all possible—always striving to reach the point at which I am ready to forgive.

# Try This

1. *Reflect on some circumstance or condition that is making you angry. Consider how to channel your anger into helpful activities that will remedy the situation.*

2. *If you are harboring resentment towards another person, strengthen your spirit by reading and reflection until you are able to forgive the person from your heart. Do this as a favor to yourself, if you can't think of any better reason.*

# Day 65—Fearlessly Seek the Truth

*Seek truth and pardon error. —Voltaire*

The fact is, I can only fully embrace life by continually and earnestly pursuing the truth—continually seeking to enfold anything that I newly discover to be true into the framework of my philosophy. I am continually rearranging my thinking to accommodate new insights that continually come to me from a variety of sources.

Part of this journey has come through the discovery of the truly awesome extent of my ignorance. When I was 13, I knew everything because I didn't know what I didn't know. And how could I?

I grew up in a conservative Christian environment and was convinced as a young man that what I was hearing was the only possible version of the truth. Anyone who disagreed with the opinions that I had come to by age 13 were ignorant of the knowledge that I had come to, or too stupid to understand the truth that I comprehended so clearly, or were possessed of an evil heart that wouldn't accept the world as I so clearly understood it to be. Twelve years of higher education and five decades of wondering, reading, listening, and learning served to bring into focus the actual extent of my ignorance.

I am a life-long learner and go to Wikipedia for one thing or another five times a day. So at any given moment I know more than I knew even a day earlier, but I feel that my knowledge only grows by addition whereas my understanding of the things that I am ignorant about grows my multiplication and, as a result, my little island of knowledge grows constantly less significant in the midst of the unbounded ocean of those things that I now know that I know nothing about.

While working on a PhD at Michigan State University, I took a graduate class that focused on the esoteric topic of The Sociology of Physics Research Centers. The class was taught by an older couple who had dedicated their lives to researching this arcane subject. I had an epiphany at one point and afterwards said to the professor, "I have known for a long time that nobody could become a Renaissance man, knowing everything there was to know. However, I just realized that you couldn't be a Renaissance man if you limited your definition of the universe to Physics." I'll never forget that moment. The professor smiled at me and said, "Don, you couldn't be a Renaissance man if you limited your definition of the universe to the Sociology of Physics Research Centers."

I have come to realize that anybody who believes that they know a lot really does have an awful lot to learn. Even the most brilliant person among us is walking with an intellectual shamble. My awareness of the limitation of my knowledge provides a great basis for my practice of Voltaire's advice in this instruction's key quote. Consciousness of the extent of my own ignorance makes it easy to pardon other people's errors—or, with any kind of smug assurance, to even label them "errors."

The French Jesuit Theologian, Pasquier Quesnel, made the accurate observation, "The truth only irritates those it enlightens, but does not convert." I am trying never to be irritated by the truth, but to engage in the pursuit of knowledge and wisdom with heart and soul—willing to go with open heart and open mind in whatever happy direction the truth may lead. I don't care what the truth is. For all my limitations, I just want to know the truth.

# Try This

1.   *Make a fearless assessment of your own willingness to accept a truth that contradicts what you have always believed to be true.*

2.   *Determine that you will always remain teachable.*

DR. DONALD HUNTINGTON

# Part III

## Practice Gracious Deeds and Behaviors

*Henry David Thoreau advised us to, "Be not simply good; be good for something." The main purpose for adding wisdom to the foundation of character is to enable you to live positively in the world. The following instructions will provide specific actions you can take, plus examples of those actions, in actually becoming good for yourself, good for others, and good for Heaven's sake.*

# Day 66—Reach out to Beautiful Things

*The best and most beautiful things in the world cannot be seen or even touched. They must be felt with the heart.*
*–Helen Keller*

Complete engagement with the things of the spirit and in relationships with people around me require me to be in touch with our feelings.

Helen Keller, the author of this instruction's key quote, was an expert on feeling. She was both blind and deaf so her sense of touch was her only channel of communication with the world. It is extraordinary, therefore, that Helen Keller should be able to speak brilliantly about the beauty of things that cannot be touched as well as about those things that not even people who possessed the gift of sight could see with their eyes. She could only have made such a leap because of the power of her indomitable human spirit, which was a beautiful thing indeed. Her spirit was itself one of the untouchable, unseeable realities she spoke about; the story of the triumph of Helen Keller over her limitations is more beautiful than any of the sunsets that she was unable to see.

I understand the truth of Keller's observation about the limitation of our senses but might suggest that the world of the senses serves its highest role in bringing to our attention those things that "must be felt with the heart." Visible beauties of nature surround my Northern California Home. We drive by Mount Diablo on a daily basis and the mountain offers a limitless variety of presentations, each of them compelling and beautiful. Magnificent people surround me, as well. Many of them wouldn't take first place in a beauty contest, but I enjoy being in their presence—observing mannerisms that so easily endear them to me. Everybody really is "beautiful in their own way." The hippies were right about that. My wife has a way of tilting her head when she laughs that I never tire of seeing. Even if I became blind, I would never despair as long as I could hold my wife in my arms. I have learned the happy principle of loving the people I can love, touching the ones I can reach, and letting the others go. I am living by Charles Dickens' cheerful dictum that I "have a heart that never hardens... and a touch that never hurts."

# How to Put Your Whole Self In

The most important realities are those invisible connections that bind us to the world of the spirit—maintaining us in a matrix of existence that draws us into an unbreakable connection with our Creator and into inescapable relationship with everyone around us. In the book *The Shack* God Almighty makes a memorable appeal:

> Rather than a pyramid, I want to be the center of a mobile,
> where everything in your life—your friends, family,
> occupation, thoughts, activities—is connected to me but moves
> with the wind, in and out and back and forth, in an incredible
> dance of being. (William P. Young)

I have come to the critical realization that the most important role my senses can play is to reaffirm for my heart those invisible realities that underlie the world that I see and touch—to throw myself without reservation into the "incredible dance of being" to which the passage refers.

Mount Diablo becomes most important to me when the sight of its looming presence lifts my heart to worship the One who made both Diablo and me. When my sense of commitment increases by seeing my wife smile, or my awareness of my role in the universe quickens by my grandchild's hug, then the things I see and touch actually assist me in feeling "with my heart," as Helen Keller put it, "the best and most beautiful things in the world."

# Try This

1. *Meditate for a few moments upon a beautiful scene or person that has lifted your heart.*

2. *Let your appreciation of the scene or the person lead you to a renewed awareness of the unseen realities that surround you.*

# Day 67—Relate to Others for Mercy's Sake

*We shall show mercy, but we shall not ask for it.*
*—Winston Churchill*

Showing mercy to others becomes one of the best ways of putting my whole self into becoming good for myself, for others, and for Heaven's sake. Shakespeare made a memorable comment about the advantages of showing mercy when he penned the famous words:

*The quality of mercy is not strained*
*It droppeth as the gentle rain from heaven*
*Upon the place beneath: it is twice blest,—*
*It blesseth him that gives and him that takes....*

Showing mercy towards another really does have the advantages that Shakespeare spoke about. As he was led to the place of execution, following a year in an English dungeon, Sir Thomas Moore saw that his executioner was nervous. Showing mercy to the man who was about to cut off his head, Moore turned to him and said, "Be not afraid, for you send me to God." How much better to face death by showing mercy, as Moore did, than to die while crying and begging for mercy or while screaming terrible curses at the headsman!

We don't have to await death to begin learning to live like this. Robert Fulghum, the author of the famous essay *All I Need to Know I Learned in Kindergarten*, once wrote about a gift he had received in a traffic situation. He said that he had stopped at a red light and, engrossed in some reflection, completely missed the fact that the light turned green until it turned back to red. Fulghum said that sitting behind him at the traffic light was a large cement truck. The driver of the truck gave him the gift of not blaring his air horn in angered frustration at this "day-dreaming, fog-bound idiot." Instead, the driver, with a heavenly display of patience, gave Fulghum the gift of simply waiting patiently until the light once again turned green.

If I were the driver of the cement truck, I am not sure I could have shown mercy at that level. What I do know, however, is that the anonymous truck driver that day illustrated a level of maturity and mercy that I ought to show. I am sure of that because he illustrated the level of mercy that I wish other people would show towards me.

I am also certain that whoever that truck driver was, he digested his lunch better, slept better that night, got along with his fellow workers better, and was happier with his wife and children, and probably even with the family dog because of the fact that during the day he was able to show an extreme level of mercy.

Mercy is the quality that is completely missing from every act of road rage, which is caused by people who are not able to be generous and merciful to the people sharing the road with them.

The fact is, it really doesn't hurt to show mercy. On the contrary, it blesses us when we give it and blesses those who receive it, just as Shakespeare said it would. He got it right. "It blesseth him that gives...." I mean, it really does! How grateful I should be if I were able to experience mercy "from heaven" to the extent that there is no one whom I wouldn't show mercy if given the opportunity to do so. What perfect freedom it would it be to not insist upon mercy from anyone in the world! A goal for my life is to continually seek to live at that level!

# Try This

1. *Show mercy today to at least one person by replacing an angry response or biting criticism with gentleness and affection.*

2. *Note what that display of mercy does in elevating your own spirit.*

# Day 68—Love the Mob

*He treated the whole mob of men as a mob of kings.*
*—GK Chesterton about Saint Francis*

When we go to San Francisco my wife, Rae, sometimes carries a pocket full of change for the panhandlers. I used to regard these people with disdain—hurrying past them, not looking at them, and wishing not to encourage their beggarly activities. I am gradually learning from Rae to hold these people with the regard that I ought to have for everyone, acknowledging the dignity and respect that belongs to them as kings of the earth made in the image of their Creator.

On a San Francisco sidewalk, Rae handed a buck to a scruffy street musician and greeted him in a friendly fashion. The man shared with her that she was the first person of all the hundreds who had passed that day who ever showed the slightest awareness that he was a human being. At another point that same day Rae turned back to a street person we had just passed to give him a handful of change. The man was so grateful to her! He complimented her on a flower she was wearing in her lapel. Then he shared an interesting story of how he had come into possession of a rose a short time before and how the rose had remained fresh and lovely for a whole week. As we turned to go, the man told Rae "Goodbye," and blessed her in God's name.

I am beginning to realize that we have a wonderful gift to give to street people. Along with a dollar bill or a handful of change, we can give them the gift of acknowledging them as human beings. We can promote them for a short time from being non-entities to becoming people with faces. At least for a moment we can provide them an opportunity to be human with us. For that brief time we at least open ourselves to doing something more to ease the difficult journey of these troubled human beings.

One of the signs indicating that I really am putting my whole self into the people around me should be easy acceptance of others regardless of their status or personal characteristics. I should be as uncaring of other people's shortcomings as I am hard on my own. No matter what terrible choices another person might have made, I can realize that I have done awful things myself—even if the results might not have been as public.

A wise observer of the human condition, Ouida Sebestyen, made the

# How to Put Your Whole Self In

accurate observation that "Indifference is the invisible giant of the world." The architect and inventor Buckminster Fuller stretched Ouida's proverb into a cosmic challenge when he wrote,

> We are not going to be able to operate our Spaceship Earth successfully nor for much longer unless we see it as a whole spaceship and our fate as common. It has to be everybody or nobody.

Our little acts of humanity serve to improve our performance as crewmembers on Spaceship Earth. Maybe the kingdom of the spirit comes not through the blare of trumpets or some invincible surmise, but through small deeds such as giving a homeless person a friendly greeting and a dollar.

I am so grateful for Rae's small but important witness before me of how love can be shared with people whom others may regard as unlovely. These are little acts, but with huge—possibly eternal—implications. The Master once said that He was homeless so I am going to try to treat the next homeless person I meet as a king incognito, as in the key quote for this instruction.

If I can't love perfectly like Jesus would, I can at least treat people like Saint Francis treated them; I can love others as Rae loves them.

# Try This

1. *Find a person in your life that needs some love and perform some loving act for him/her.*

2. *For one day make a deliberate effort to demonstrate a loving attitude towards everyone you meet.*

# Day 69—Hug Your Way into Health

*For human beings, you need two hugs a day to survive, four hugs for maintenance, six hugs to grow. —Virginia Satir*

There's almost no more direct way of putting my whole self into the consciousness of other people than to give them a big hug. I don't bother with a little squeeze, I hold people to myself and give them a chance to learn that at that moment I am giving them all the love that I have in my heart.

A university professor, Dr. Leo Buscaglia, was stunned when one of his brightest young students committed suicide. As a preventive measure against future repeats, he began to line his students up to give them each a big hug before and after each class. "If somebody hugs you, you know you must be there or they'll go through you," Buscaglia said.

Some people think hugging to be childish. In fact, children really love to hug and to touch. When he was seven, my grandchild would hug cabin attendants when boarding airplanes and other children he would meet in the mall. He periodically gave hugs to everyone in whatever room he was in that made them all feel like they had been touched by an angel. Hugging is not childish, even though the practice has some child-like qualities. In the moment of an embrace two people become like children for a moment, deliberately dropping defenses that we adults keep in place all the rest of the time.

My grandchild and I are both non-discriminating huggers of men, women, children, senior citizens (who are some of the most fun people to hug), laughing people, grieving, joyful, dying…. The only people I don't hug on a regular basis are young women because they sometimes think that getting a hug from an old guy is too weird. I also am careful about this around people of Asian descent with a cultural bias against this level of physical contact that I try to respect. I have also learned to respect the wishes of some individuals—especially guys—who just don't like to be touched, but most people I meet are glad to be hugged, or at least they learn to be glad. One woman told me that the first time I met her and her husband I gave them both a big hug. She said her husband asked her afterwards, "Why did that guy hug me?" Now she says he's disappointed if he misses his hug.

Most of all, I hug and touch my wife. Rae and I have been married for 44 years and often hold hands when we drive in the car. I hug her the first time we are both conscious in the morning, hug her last thing before we go to sleep at night, and typically hug her whenever our paths cross during the day.

Albert Schweitzer made the poignant statement: "We are all so much together and yet we are all dying of loneliness." Touching and hugging provides a curative for psychological isolation, which is one of modern society's most terrible illnesses. I know a few people consider hugging to be a strange custom of mine, but everyone knows after I have hugged them that I have hugged them good. I hug them beyond social convention. Many accept it as a gift—which they usually give right back to me.

"Six hugs a day to grow," the key quote for this instruction says. If ever I am feeling spiritually stunted, I can simply find someone and give him or her a big bear hug. The experience improves my spiritual health and adds an inch or so to my spiritual height and to the height of the person I hugged.

# Try This

1. *Give a hug to at least six people when you meet today; use both arms, hug them close. Hold them for a moment. Don't tell them you have a hugging plan; tell them that you are glad to be with them.*

2. *If you are married or have a significant other, be sure to hug him/her at least morning, noon, and night.*

# Day 70—Make Others Feel Great

*There is a great man who makes every man feel small. But the real great man is the man who makes every man feel great.*
*–G.K. Chesterton*

An important quality in putting one's whole self into the challenge of relating to others is the intention of helping others feel like they are worthwhile and even admirable. There is no manipulation about this for me, since the people around me really do have qualities that should rightly arouse the admiration of anyone who would take time to discover and acknowledge them.

I am on the receiving end of that kind of acknowledgment. For example, I am technologically deficient but my buddy, Dan "The Guru" Shafer, knows more facts about more topics than anyone I ever met. He is the author of more than 60 books on technology topics. Even in technology rich Silicon Valley, some people regarded Dan as the person with answers. He is an awesome storehouse of ideas and knowledge. Even though Dan is better informed about almost everything than I am, he has treated me with deference and graciousness during all the decades that we have known each other. He always makes me feel like I am a better person than I actually am. Several people in this world, like Dan, make me feel great. My buddy, Pete, is a talented graphics design person who has never said a single depreciating word about my astounding lack of artistic skill. He always gives me the impression that I could be an artist with a little effort.

Every day I encounter people who astound me. My partner and business manager has a genius for relating to other people. The writers whom I ghostwrite for continually dazzle me with the lives they have led and the talents they have brought to the challenges of living. The truth is that I am surrounded by individuals with stories and lives that grip me and inspire me because I am bending my ear to catch their stories and looking intently to see with comprehension the significance of the lives of the people with whom I am encountering.

I know that my writings about people in my magazine and ghostwriting projects—based as they are on my love and admiration for each of them—become sources of psychic strength, encouragement, and self-worth. It is easy for those people to feel great about themselves, because they know that I am aware of their greatness; they can admire themselves through the lens of my admiration. I continually discover that having this kind of attitude towards others elevates me, as well.

I once told my friend, Cristina, that some people must be couch potatoes who stumble through life with nothing remarkable ever going on in their spirit, but that I couldn't think of any offhand. I'll never forget Cristina's response. "Don," she said to me, "If we ever have patience to get through the noise and static going on in the lives of such people, we would always be able to catch a little flute-like melody that might fill us with delight." I was so thankful for Cristina's wise comment! She really is one of the "great" people referred to in Chesterton's quote. I am trying to share in her view towards others; looking for the opportunity to cherish and to admire the smallest "flute-note" of greatness that I can catch from them.

I live in the midst of so many wonderful people—many of them trying, sometimes successfully, to help me feel good about myself. Because of them I do feel great! While living like this, how could I feel otherwise?

# Try This

1.  *For the next 24 hours—to the extent that you can do so— identify something you can admire in every person you meet.*

2.  *As appropriate, share with each person the thing that you admire and then cherish the sense that you receive about how your comment warmed each of them and made you feel great about yourself.*

# Day 71—Don't Strike Back

*We are not at peace with others because we are not at peace
with ourselves. And we are not at peace with others because we
are not at peace with God. —Thomas Merton*

The act of offering my life in complete service to the people around
me and to Heaven presumes living free from the corrosive effects of such
dark emotions as hatred, antagonism, resentment, and rage—those negative
qualities that destroy my peace and that cause me to strike out at another
person, or at least wish to do so. Therefore, the driving need to be at peace
with others is one of the most important issues in putting my whole self into
life. As Merton's quote points out, the basis for any peace in my life is first to
be at peace with Heaven. Oswald Chambers wrote the stirring words:

> *If the outer level of our spiritual life with God is impaired to
> the slightest degree, we must put everything else aside until we
> make it right. Remember that spiritual vision depends on our
> character.*

Righteous anger is hardly ever a useful tool. Such anger is positive in
the context of such things as reacting towards such things as a violent home
invasion, an animal that is attacking a child, or towards a cruel attack on
anyone. When a man approaches my wife with a raised club, it is time for me
to take a break from my calm attitude. However, how often have I actually
found myself in the kind of situation that would justify a furious response?
How many times has someone around me actually been attacked? Verbal
attacks are far more common, but unlike physical attacks, a calm response is
the best way to counter a verbal offense. "A soft answer turns away wrath,"
runs an old proverb. When a soft answer is not readily available, I can always
just let things pass.

Following some exchange a fellow worker once said to me, "Don, you
don't even know when you've been insulted." Well, the truth was that I knew
the comment, whatever it was, could have been taken as an insult. But what's
the point? It never accomplishes any good to trade insults with anybody, nor
to leap to my own defense.

I should be more willing to defend someone else against a verbal attack
of some kind, but even then, a calm and reasonable response will almost always

be more effective than a thousand curses and counter insults.

How free from inappropriate anger do I actually need to be before the grace of God has perfect access to my life? In other words: How much rage in my life is too much rage? The question is similar to asking: How much battery acid can you put in lemonade before there is too much battery acid? Or: How many rats can a homemaker have in a kitchen before there are too many rats? The Master told me, "Be perfect, therefore, as your heavenly Father is perfect." This is obviously an absolute standard for my purity. My inner spirit must be calm in the face of whatever outrages I may be facing.

A standard of purity like the one that the Bible demands, of course, is far beyond my ability to comply with. I finally discovered the wonderful experience that when the sunshine of Heaven shines into my heart, it kills the moral vermin of evil attitudes and responses to others that otherwise would mar my life. I don't need to be a person of peace in any sense in order to open myself up to His sunshine, I only need to take the lid off of my life—exposing all the dark places and the hidden corners—and letting the sunshine do its work, chasing the vermin that might be there deep into their holes.

I don't even have to try very hard to be good! I just keep the lid of my spirit open to the sun above me—receiving Heaven's forgiveness and filling my life with the power of His life and light. Because I'm at peace with God, harmony with others becomes a natural outcome.

I still become annoyed, but not very often. Moreover, the episodes usually conclude with a confession of my failure and a renewed determination that, by the help of Heaven, I'll become a man of indomitable peace.

# Try This

1. *Today through prayer and meditation, open yourself up to the sunshine of God's peace.*

2. *With a heart filled with that sunshine, practice indomitable peace with everyone you meet.*

DR. DONALD HUNTINGTON

# Day 72—Live Above Desperation

*Nowadays most men lead lives of noisy desperation.*
*–James Thurber*

Thurber's quote obviously puts a wry spin on Thoreau's famous declaration of people living "lives of *quiet* desperation." The contrast is appropriate because Thoreau lived in a world that was much quieter than the one that Thurber occupied a century later, following the advent of such things as radio, television, stereo systems, internal combustion motors, and jet-powered airplanes. Thurber died in 1961 and didn't live to see the noisy desperation become buried even further beneath the racket generated by iPods, CD players, and Internet radios. Cable television especially fills our ears and minds with the sounds of gunfire, canned laughter, full-color carnage, hemorrhoid cures, groping sexual encounters, and political sound bites—none of which encourages me to engage in life and to participate in deliberate service for others, but merely provides a soporific that dulls my spirit and distracts me from acknowledging the emptiness of my life.

Eliminating the root causes of desperation frees me from any need to fill my ears and mind with clamor and clatter. I find myself often sitting in a room with the television set turned off or driving down the road with my car radio silent. Remaining connected with The Source of spiritual energy delivers me from many problems and battles that formerly made me desperately seek for some distraction. The connection enables me to undergo a daily transformation! Every day I feel again like the sun in King David's poetic description of the sunrise; I become, "like a bridegroom coming forth from his pavilion, like a champion rejoicing to run his course."

The world is in desperate need of seeing examples of lives that are not desperate. I am determined to be a man of peace; to remain patient and calm in the midst of chaos and turmoil; to be a rock of serenity beneath which troubled people can take refuge. Mark Twain wrote that calmness is "a language that even the deaf can hear and the blind can read." That calming language is the most effective dialect in which to speak the words of compassion as well as affection.

# How to Put Your Whole Self In

One of the central characteristics of a life awash in grace is this pronounced quality of peacefulness or, as Mark Twain refers to it, "calmness." The word "peace" sometimes gives the impression of an absence of turbulence or strife. In that sense, peace isn't the right word for our troubled lives. Perhaps the word "calmness" refers exactly to the quality that comes from my response to any troubles when I remain connected to The Source of my strength. If peacefulness were depended only upon circumstances, I would often be living life with a very unsettled, troubled heart, since storms and turbulence are as natural a part of my life as they are a part of nature. My connection to Heaven creates a place of calm directly in the midst of any storm that might come blowing through my life.

I find that, remarkably, I now have an ability to remain calm during a stormy period! Perhaps my life can be pictured more like a hurricane than a thunderstorm. A thunderstorm is full of sound and fury from one side to the other. However, the eye of a hurricane has a peaceful place at its core where the sun shines and hardly a breeze blows. In the same way, it seems, deep inside myself, right at the center of my being, there is a quiet place that cannot be disturbed no matter how fiercely the winds of life may blow around the edges.

The Source of all goodness is waiting to bestow upon me the gifts of His presence and His power. No longer will I be too distracted to reflect upon that presence or to receive those gifts.

# Try This

1. *Consider the times during the past three-to-four days when you were least desperate or especially fulfilled. What were you doing at those times?*

2. *Now think of ways to replicate the conditions that brought you the degree of peace you identified in question #1.*

# Day 73—Just Show Up

*Eighty percent of success is showing up.* –Woody Allen

An important part of putting my whole self into becoming good for myself, good for others, and good for Heaven's sake lies in simply following Woody Allen's wise advice to just show up every day. Almost every good thing that has come to me has been the result of the grace of Heaven mixing with some level of persistence or faithfulness on my part. I need to be consistent and persistent! To be dependable! Relationships in my life flourish or wither to the extent that I continue "showing up" for people or absenting myself in some way.

George Matheson learned Hebrew and Greek, memorized great sections of the Bible, and could speak so capably in public that audiences were often unaware of the fact that he was completely blind. Matheson claimed that his success was based upon:

> ...the power to work under stress; to have a great weight at your heart and still run; to have a deep anguish in your spirit and still perform the daily tasks.... The hardest thing is that most of us are called to exercise our patience, not in the sickbed but in the street.

The Bible says that a healthy spiritual life produces the qualities of love, joy, peace, patient endurance, kindness, goodness, faithfulness, gentleness, and self-control (Galatians 5:22-23). That third quality, "patient endurance," was in one sense the most important because without discipline a person couldn't have any of the other characteristics in very great measure; if I permit the winds of my feelings to blow me here and there, I can't effectively love; my life will be joyless, chaotic, troubled, and so forth. The American social reformer, photographer, and journalist, Jacob Riis, once wrote:

> I look at a stonecutter hammering away at a rock 100 times without so much as a crack showing in it. Yet at the 101st blow it splits in two. I know it was not the one blow that did it, but all that had gone before.

The Bible gives us a promise, "Let us not become weary in doing good, for at the proper time we will reap a harvest if we do not give up." (Gal. 6:9).

## How to Put Your Whole Self In

I know my heart! I have been married to the same person for more than 40 years, but I'll freely admit that I am no stronger in mind and will than most divorced people that I am acquainted with. Based on my own strength I could never continue to do the things I know I ought to do. I would have been divorced long ago; I would probably be living in a van somewhere on government assistance. A quality of grace in my life lifts me above the circumstances of my limited spiritual powers. I often recite to myself an ancient promise:

> *He gives strength to the weary and increases the power of the weak. Even youths grow tired and weary, and young men stumble and fall; but those who hope in the LORD will renew their strength. They will soar on wings like eagles; they will run and not grow weary, they will walk and not be faint.*

I want to be persistent and consistent in my life, but not as plodding drudgery. I want to fly! I want to soar! By the energy that Heaven shares with me, I will continue to do good. I am determined to keep on keeping on for the rest of my life. I am going to show up today, for sure.

# Try This

1. *Make a list of the things that you want to accomplish today; sort the items from most important to least important.*

2. *Start on the list. Don't quit before you are finished with at least the most important items at the top of the list. "Show up" in the most important ways today.*

# Day 74—Fearlessly Engage in Life

*Only through experience of trial and suffering can the soul be strengthened, ambition inspired, and success achieved.*
*–Helen Keller*

Helen Keller seemingly engaged with life at a deeper level than anyone would have imagined possible, overcoming the nightmarish experience of becoming both deaf and blind before age two. Even now, I can scarcely believe that she not only learned to speak and to write, but earned a bachelor's degree, became a media darling, and eventually developed into an effective champion for peace, women's rights, workers' rights, and other causes that fired her heart. Keller threw herself wholeheartedly into life, beginning with her response to the staggering loss that she suffered before becoming fully conscious.

"When we do the best that we can, we never know what miracle is wrought in our life, or in the life of another," she said. Helen Keller herself became the best example of miracles being "wrought" through the lives of people who do their best.

Many of us imagine that we are doing our "best" when, in fact, we are operating only at a tiny fraction of the actual performance level that would be possible if we only, somehow, could learn to put our whole selves into making the most of the opportunities that come our way. Perhaps the radical difference between the success that Keller enjoyed and the limited accomplishments that most of us settle for is that she transformed her blindness into positive energy. Rather than viewing her sufferings as limitations, she used problems as springboards to enable her to engage more fully in life.

"I can see, and that is why I can be happy in what you call the dark," she wrote, "but which to me is golden." Then she added the explanation, "I can see a God-made world, not a manmade world." The quote shows how Keller actually used her blindness as a basis for creating an amazing world of her imagination—providing her with resources and visions that filled her with energy and motivation for engaging the world at a complete level; she was able to see within herself a shining image that apparently illuminated pathways leading to her remarkable accomplishments.

# How to Put Your Whole Self In

The actor and comedian Jim Carrey made a wise observation: "I don't think human beings learn anything without desperation." But in spite of that, through timidity and dread, we often desperately make choices to pull back and to not persevere in activities or projects that might have blessed ourselves and blessed others if we had only channeled the problems and challenges into positive directions rather than by retreating from things that we really ought to do.

Keller was able to channel her insights and apply the salutary power of troubles and loss in order to instill within herself the courage to confront problems without flinching. "Avoiding danger is no safer in the long run than outright exposure," she said—and then added, "Life is a daring adventure or nothing at all."

"Although the world is full of suffering, it is full also of the overcoming of it," she said. I can picture her smiling broadly as she said it. I am determined to follow the upward path that Keller showed to me. I am never again going to use troubles and even suffering as reasons to pull back from life; I'll never use difficulties as excuses for not following down the bright pathways that Heaven or destiny beckons me to follow.

# Try This

1. *On a piece of paper write a problem that is holding you back from achieving your dreams and goals.*

2. *Imagine a plan for overcoming the problem that will actually turn it to your advantage.*

# Day 75—Let Others Spit on You

*In the end these things matter most: How well did you love?*
*How fully did you love? How deeply did you learn to let go?*
*—Buddha*

Putting my whole self into life requires me to develop the ability to face hostility with tranquility and not to permit anybody's angry judgmental attitudes to find even the smallest response in my own spirit.

Two men were riding on an elevator. The car stopped at a floor and a third man got on. He walked up to one of the passengers, deliberately spat on him, and then got off at the next floor. As the man wiped off the saliva with his handkerchief, he showed no sign of anger nor gave any indication that he had found it in the least disturbing to have another person spit on him. "What's the matter with you!" shouted the other passenger. "How can you just let another person do something like that to you without getting upset?"

"That guy has big problems," the man answered. "I am unwilling to share any of his issues nor grant him the ability to disturb my serenity."

We can't do anything in life without attracting enemies. While he was alive a number of people considered Abraham Lincoln to be an evil misguided fool. Some Christians believed that Billy Graham was doing the work of the devil. Most of all, of course, Jesus Christ was put to death by His enemies. I know there are people who don't like me and who speak evil of me. Such reports don't shake me because, after all, having enemies never fazed my Master's sense of serenity. People spat upon Him! "Father forgive them," He prayed as He went to His death at their hands. Then He added a rationale for the forgiveness "They know not what they do." Jesus was aware, of course, that appalling ignorance lies behind every judgmental act.

My attitude of forgiveness must have nothing to do with whether a person necessarily deserves or even particularly desires my forgiveness. I try to forgive everybody because otherwise sinister forces of resentment and unforgiving attitudes will absolutely cast down the sense of joy and peace that rightfully belong upon the throne of my heart. After all, nobody in this world needs my forgiveness more than I need forgiveness from myself. If I can only accomplish that monumental task, then it should be easy to forgive anybody else for anything.

## How to Put Your Whole Self In

I discovered long ago that even the worst people often have characteristics that I can respect or, in many cases, esteem. As a result, I deliberately attempt to look for things to admire and even cherish about everyone I meet. If I can make the offender a person I admire, then it is a piece of cake to not take offense.

Will Rogers said, "I never met a man I didn't like." These days I know just what he meant. It wasn't that he and I have never found someone who wasn't worthy of being disliked, but we simply made up our minds that we were going to like people without making a judgment whether they were worthy of our affection or not. I am not half the man that Will Rogers was, but I am determined to keep the clean light of the love that I am living in these days undimmed by any shadows of animosity that I might hold against anyone in this world. People couldn't make me hate them by spitting on me.

Loving unlovely people is the way anybody can bring a small part of heaven down to earth. The will to love anyone no matter how unlovable can lead to miracles.

# Try This

1. *Show affection in some way to a person whom you don't naturally love. If rebuffed, seek another opportunity. Continue to do this until successful.*

2. *Observe carefully the differences your attitude and behavior makes in the relationship.*

# Day 76—Take Advantage of Reciprocating Generosity

*I have come to believe that giving and receiving are really the same. Giving and receiving—not giving and taking.*
*–Joyce Grenfell*

"Give and you will receive," the Master told us. And then to drive the promise home, He added a robust and poetic description of the kind of receiving that the person who followed His principle would receive: "Good measure, pressed down, and shaken together shall men pour into your lap" (Luke 6:38). Some preachers maintain that faith in God will open doors to personal wealth and power. It is limiting and wrong-hearted to regard—even in the back of our minds—any act of charity to be a technique for self-aggrandizement. The actual truth—that I have demonstrated so many times in my own life—is the simple principle that people tend to be generous in response to generosity.

Many years ago I made a contract with God that if anyone would ever say any variation of the words, "Don, I need to ask you for a favor...." I would always answer "Yes I will," before the person had an opportunity to tell me what they were asking for. If the request happened to be something that I was unable to do, I would simply give the reason for not being able to comply. However, if it was something I was able to do, I would just do it. Just for nothing. Do it just for the love of the person and for the love of Heaven.

Most people would be frightened of doing that—fearful that the person might ask something that they would be unwilling or unable to do. However, I have discovered that life takes care of me, somehow, when I simply throw myself wholeheartedly into the act of living—and especially into the act of living for others. During the 15 years or so that I have been doing that, never once did a person ask me to do something that I really didn't want to do. It has seemed to me, of course, that this was simply God keeping His part of the bargain. Beyond that, I think, is the simple principle that people tend to behave as you expect them to. I expected that people would not take advantage of my generosity and they never did. Not once that I can remember!

# How to Put Your Whole Self In

We limit and even destroy relationships by trying to protect ourselves from people wishing to take advantage of us. By God, I want people to take advantage of me. I want to put my whole self into helping others. When people say things like, "I hate to ask you to take me to the airport so late at night, I sometimes respond with a line, "I love you. I would kill for you or die for you—or take you to the airport." The line never fails to make the person laugh. The act of happy subjection alerts them to the principle that is at work in the relationship. I am doing something for them; but I am experiencing the joy of service that comes out of that act. In every case, I feel that I am getting more out of the transaction than I am putting in.

This is invariably true because the quote for this instruction is a statement of the way the moral universe actually operates. I will ruin the beautiful thing by ever trying to take anything for myself. By giving simply, freely, and without reservation I really do receive more than I can ever give.

# Try This

1. *The next time anyone asks for a favor, tell them you'll be glad to do it before they inform you what the favor is.*

2. *Watch the reaction. See what happens in their heart and in your own.*

# Day 77—Lift People Up

*Let us make one point, that we meet each other with a smile,
when it is difficult to smile. Smile at each other, make time for
each other in your family. –Mother Teresa*

C.S. Lewis once observed that if you don't like someone, you should treat the person exactly as you would if you, in fact, loved him/her very much. In most cases, Lewis said, you will end up with the feelings you are imitating. I think the kind of gentle dissimulation Lewis advocates is tough for many people. The process of putting our whole selves into life and of becoming good for something in this world requires us to access resources of grace—those sources of positive energy that lie outside ourselves.

We all know people who lack any desire to be pleasant when it is difficult to do so. Mother Teresa's advice actually works best for people like herself—people who are awash in grace. Moreover, it should be understood that the lives of people marked by grace are also marked by love. Following Mother Teresa's standard doesn't mean that I am required to like everyone. I don't even have to pretend to like people who have abused me or who behave in unpleasant ways. Decades ago a comment by C.S. Lewis changed forever my attitude about accepting other people:

> *Try to understand exactly what loving your neighbor as
> yourself means. I have to love him as I love myself. Well, how
> exactly do I love myself? Now that I come to think of it, I have
> not exactly got a feeling of fondness or affection for myself,
> and I do not even always enjoy my own society. So apparently
> "Love your neighbor" does not mean "feel fond of him" or "find
> him attractive..." That is an enormous relief.*

Decades have passed since I first read that, but I can still remember my own sense of relief and even delight at those words. Even if I don't like some of the people around me, I can love them with the love that even selfish people reserve for themselves.

Lewis' quote puts a great spin on the requirement—necessitated by my goal of putting my whole self into the processes of living—to be gracious towards people who commit unlovely or even harmful acts. I freely admit that I am one of the unlovely people I have to get along with. I have done things that make me angry disappointed, puzzled, and dismayed at myself. Don Huntington has caused me more difficulties than all the other people in the world combined.

It is only reasonable, if I love you as I love myself that I will then treat you the same way that I tend to treat myself. I am not going to gossip about you. I am going to try to view your actions in the most favorable possible light. I intend to leap to your defense every time I am given the opportunity to do so. When people say something negative about you, I am going to try to say something positive.

I don't do that perfectly, of course. Perhaps I don't even do it usually. Nevertheless, I do it sometimes and I intend to get better at it—to treat others as I wish they would treat me; to treat them as I treat myself. In some cases, I'll even treat them far better than I treat myself. I am upset with some things I do that I completely disregard or instantly forgive in anyone else. Putting myself into service for others is always rewarding.

# Try This

1.  *Identify the person in your life with whom you are most aggravated. List 2-5 things you might do for that person if you sincerely loved him/her.*

2.  *Keep doing them for a week. At the end of the week analyze the changes in your heart and spirit that you have experienced.*

# Day 78—Clean the Cheese off Your Mustache

*As long as a man stands in his own way, everything seems to be in his way.* –Ralph Waldo Emerson

Life offers its best gifts to me when I am prepared to meet it armed with the right attitudes and appropriate behaviors.

A man once stole into a friend's hotel room in the middle of the night and smeared Limburger cheese on the man's mustache. When the friend awoke he sniffed his sheets and said, "These bedclothes stink!" He arose and stood in the middle of his room, sniffed the air, and said, "This room stinks!" Getting dressed he walked out of his door, sniffed the air again, and said, "This hallway stinks!" Entering the foyer of the hotel, he sniffed again and said, "This whole hotel stinks!" Then the man walked out of the hotel, sniffed the air, and shouted, "The whole world stinks!"

There have been times when I really believed that the whole world had an evil smell when the real problem was my stinking attitude. Reflecting upon the state of my own heart turned out to be more important that using a mirror to reflect the condition of my appearance. Once I had addressed the root problem, and cleaned the Limburger cheese off of my spiritual mustache the whole world changed.

Identifying a problem is half the job of fixing it. A great step to realize that I am responsible for most of the bad things in my life:

- My wife wasn't an irritable woman; I was an irritating man.
- My children weren't rebellious; I failed to behave in ways that earned their respect.
- My fellow-workers weren't cold and unfriendly; I wasn't a very easy person to like or even to depend upon.

The situation was improved by more than simply cleaning up my attitude. Rather than just no longer having the equivalent of smelly cheese on my mustache, I bring a pleasant savor to bear on the world, which might be the equivalent of the man in the story smearing his mustache with jasmine, lavender, or lilac. In that case, he would regard the world as a sweet-smelling place indeed. I have learned the power in the words of a Buddhist Monk:

# How to Put Your Whole Self In

*Though we all have the fear and the seeds of anger within us,
we must learn not to water those seeds and instead nourish our
positive qualities—those of compassion, understanding, and
loving kindness. (Thich Nhat Hanh)*

My reformed attitude permits me to regard the people around me as being fundamentally good—and to look at problems as simply challenges that will lead to good outcomes by such things as teaching me lessons about patience and about using difficulties for my advantage.

The wonderful thing about reformed attitudes is the power that they have to actually change circumstances. Katherine Mansfield described a certifiable truth when she wrote:

*Could we change our attitude, we should not only see life
differently, but life itself would come to be different. Life
would undergo a change of appearance because we ourselves
had undergone a change of attitude.*

I am so grateful that the same principle of grace that keeps the cheese off my spiritual mustache fills my existence with a holiday-like delight! All the elements in my life—work, recreation, family, friends, even acquaintances— are working together to transform my routine into a daily celebration. No one could imagine what living in grace is like without actually doing so. "Taste and see...," somebody said. I am tasting! Delicious!

# Try This

1. *Make it a firm policy to avoid any grimy activity that would diminish your ability to enjoy life in its purest and therefore most enjoyable terms.*

2. *Keep yourself clean by maintaining standards of purity, devotion, thrift, chastity, and integrity. These positive qualities, like healthy ingredients in a culinary dish, will create a vigorous robust joyful life experience.*

# Day 79—Leave Other People's Crackers Alone

*The Bible shows the way to go to heaven, not the way the heavens go.*

*—Galileo Galilei*

We limit the degree to which our lives can bless others by not having an appropriate sense of humility regarding the limits of our knowledge.

For example, a common fault of religious people is for us to claim more for our faith than the sources of our religious information ever claimed— causing some Christians in preceding generations to believe that they could tell from the Bible that the earth was flat. Centuries later, during Galileo's time, they believed that we could tell from the Bible that the earth not the sun is at the center of the universe. In our own time, some of us claim that we can tell from the Bible that God created the earth 7,000 years ago by a series of pronouncements rather than creating it millions of years ago by a set of processes.

We make an even worse mistake by violently arguing our version of the truth to the point of squeezing the higher qualities of peace, love, and joy out of our relationships. Some Christians argue as though the integrity of God depends upon our being able successfully to defend the Bible's truthfulness.

The marvelous author, Jeffrey Archer, once wrote a short story about a man on a subway who was offended because, while reading his paper and munching on a snack of crackers, a stranger in the next seat kept glaring at him while helping himself to the man's crackers. The passenger discovered only after he had gotten off the train that his unopened bag of crackers was still in his pocket. He himself had actually been committing the outrageous *faux pas* of helping himself to a stranger's snack. He had been so angry! Nevertheless, he was so wrong!

I know exactly how the two men in the story felt because I have occasionally been on both sides of such a misunderstanding myself. As a result, I am now trying to hold on to my opinions with a light grip. I am grateful for the immeasurable increase of joy in my life that has resulted from my still-partial victory over any need to demonstrate to other people that I am right about anything. Nobody can ever be truly joyful who hasn't learned with great good cheer to let other people be wrong—even dead wrong!

These days I am trying to keep my attitude in line with the teachings of the Bible, when it instructed us to do things that are "...excellent and profitable for everyone" and to avoid "foolish controversies ... and arguments and quarrels" (Titus 3:8-9). The philosopher Voltaire wrote the words, "Love truth, and pardon error." Voltaire, "the incomparable infidel," got a lot of things wrong, but I think he got that quote exactly right. I've learned to "pardon" errors at the drop of a hat.

I am just eating my own crackers these days. When people say things that I don't agree with, I resist jumping in to argue my own position. I cannot have real peace in my heart until I am able to permit people around me to be wrong without being upset by what I perceive as their error. To use Galileo's words from the key quote above, this is the way for me to "go to Heaven."

A main force in the reformation (perhaps 'revolution') of my attitude has come from the enormous number of times when I have been wrong myself. Just like the man with the crackers, I have been sure of myself on many occasions when I have actually been deeply in error. As a result, I am finally losing the ability to be judgmental. These days I am often escaping the condemnation of the Bible when it said:

> *You, therefore, have no excuse, you who pass judgment on someone else, for at whatever point you judge the other, you are condemning yourself, because you who pass judgment do the same things (Romans 2:1).*

Right! I have unjustly "eaten other people's crackers" so many times that I can't be too judgmental any more when they help themselves to somebody else's, or even to mine.

# Try This

1. *The next time somebody says something you disagree with—or even know to be wrong—try not saying anything to correct him/her.*

2. *Develop the habit of letting people be wrong.*

# Day 80—Do the Right Thing

*There's nothing more powerful than doing what is right even when we don't feel like it. –Joyce Meyer*

The American author and motivational speaker, Zig Ziglar, accurately noted that, "the chief cause of failure and unhappiness is trading what you want most for what you want now." I have often missed opportunities to put my whole self into life, plus missed relationships through which I could bless others and bless myself simply by making the senseless mistake of offering upon the altar of doing what I want now the sacrifice of what I really want most from my life. This especially applies to issues of ethics and morality.

The challenge was for me to become sufficiently committed to achieving my goals that my passion drives me past the temptation to waste time and resources on things that don't move me towards my goal.

I still sometimes seem to possess an innate ability to find creative ways to disengage from life. Early in my life I entertained a sneaking suspicion that useless and even forbidden pleasures are the most exciting; that attempts to be good and productive must represent boring departures from my experience of joyful and happy fun. Therefore, I laughed out loud with delight when I first encountered a great quote by C.S. Lewis:

> *Our desires are not too strong, but too weak. We are half-hearted creatures, fooling about with drink and sex and ambition, when infinite joy is offered to us, like an ignorant child who wants to go on making mud pies in the slum because he cannot imagine what is meant by the offer of a holiday at the sea. We are far too easily pleased.*

The "half-hearted" pleasures that Lewis refers to no longer seem compelling. I am resisting the shabby pleasures and heartless ambitions that beckoned in such an alluring manner that at times I couldn't imagine why I shouldn't instantly surrender myself to their charms. Television shows provide many Illustrations of what I am avoiding. If you spoke of chastity to one of the characters on Friends, Seinfeld, or Frasier, for example, they would look at you like you had dropped from space. Characteristics like purity, devotion, thrift, chastity, and integrity have always made the majority of people uncomfortable, but the current popular culture regards them with actual bewilderment. Many people today could never imagine practicing these virtues and thus missing all the fun!

The fact is that many of the "fun" things in our society are ultimately no fun at all. It's to the credit of the writers of Seinfeld that they never depicted the characters as being fulfilled and happy; they were chaotic, joyless, unloving, and unloved. Finally, of course, the whole bunch ended up in a jail cell they richly deserved. They really had spent their days "making mud pies in the slum."

I have engaged in frivolous activities that robbed my life of the power Joyce Meyer referred to in the key quote—watching television shows that don't engage my mind and heart; reading books and magazines that fail to instruct or even entertain; playing online games that don't lift me up or even amuse me; and engaging in empty relationships with people during which I would gripe, argue, and complain.

I am trying to stop wasting my time with foolish and evil distractions; concentrating on those things that really do lift my spirits, instruct me, and most of all help move me towards the life of helpful service that the Master created me to have.

# Try This

1. *Reflect upon a recent activity that you know wasted your time, diminished your life, or kept you from moving towards the goals you want to achieve.*

2. *Make a resolution not to repeat the activity. Write the resolution down.*

# Day 81—Learn to Move and to Remain Immovable

*All humanity is divided into three classes: those who are*
*immovable, those who are movable, and those who move!*
*–Benjamin Franklin*

I only put my whole self into the act of living when I can move among all three states that Franklin describes. For one thing, I want to be immovable in the sense of maintaining a positive cheerful attitude whether circumstances around me are happy or gloomy. However, I want to be movable, as well. When it comes to matters of intellect and spirit, my goal is to be like a pilgrim—always on the move and heading into new areas of contemplation, service, and learning. Perhaps what I want most of all is to be one of the movers that Franklin talked about—to be able to change the world around me forever for good. Some acts of deranged people in our society come out of this common need for significance. People who commit all-too-familiar atrocities involving bombs or guns are sometimes driven mad by the need to do something, anything, in order to exert some impact upon the world around them.

I am deliberately confronting the challenge of remaining immovable in areas that call for me to remain steadfast, movable in matters of learning and growth, while being a force in moving other people in positive directions. Successfully accomplishing the three diverse purposes requires a source of mental and spiritual energy.

A negative force within each of us is equivalent to a thermodynamic principle operating in the physical world. A process of enervation, called entropy, causes usable energy to continually diminish. Just as in the case of water always running downhill, spiritual entropy increases so that the processes of our lives run down towards stasis and doldrums unless constantly renewed by a source of energy from outside the system.

However, there is cause for hope. Water can only run down a stream but it continues running forever down the stream because, as Robert Frost reminds us, "The sun runs down in sending up the brook." And then—referring to the cycles of evaporation and rain—Frost adds the observation that there is an ultimate source of energy back of it all "that sends up the sun."

I have discovered by experience that the very same source of energy that "sends up the sun"—thereby sending up the stream—is available to keep my own life from running down to dissolution and despair. I have access to a nourishing resource—a power for living—that can maintain the little pool of my life full and running over. The power is personal. A divine Presence is operating like a fountain with overflowing nourishment for my mind and spirit. The cares and hammerings of life lose their ability to affect me very much as long as I remain connected to that internal source of renewal and healing.

The truth is that qualities such as joy, calmness, love, and gentleness often seem to be operative in my spirit with little regard either for negative circumstances or dysfunctional people. I can sometimes be kind towards people who are rude, regularly calm when conditions about me are stormy, and often peaceable in the face of confrontation.

In another sense, I am becoming constantly more movable. The stronger my practice of grace grows, the more apt I am to be moved to action by the needs of people around me. For another thing, when I realize that I have again failed in some important fashion, as I often do, the power of this overflowing grace—through forgiveness and reconciliation—is available to get me back on track.

Finally, with constantly less effort, I seem to be increasingly more "real" and more able to urge people in a positive direction than ever before.

I am grateful that my feet are planted upon a mighty Rock, which gives me a solid base upon which to stand, traction in order to progress, and leverage for helping others move ahead towards their own goals. Many days I seem to be trying less and accomplishing more than ever before in my life.

# Try This

1. *To the extent possible, every moment during the next 24 hours keep offering a prayer from your spirit, "Accept my life as a sacrifice that I offer to You."*

2. *Maintain that connection as a channel through which power can flow into you and through you as The Source works out His purposes.*

# Day 82—Treat Yourself to the Greatest Happiness

*Life's greatest happiness is to be convinced we are loved.*
*—Victor Hugo*

I am acquainted with a number of unhappy people living with desperation, anxiety, and anger. When I stray from behind the psychological and spiritual defenses I have in place, I am not above experiencing those kinds of emotions myself.

The rising incidence of road rage is one of many phenomena in our society pointing to the groundswell of unhappiness that surrounds us. Some of my liberal friends are angry and upset about the manner in which conservative forces control the media in this country. Some conservative relatives are angry and upset by the way the forces of liberalism control the media in this country.

I knew people who were so angry at President Bush—and others later at President Obama—that they could hardly keep from spitting when the name of whichever reviled president would come up. People are mad about the traffic, depressed about the price of gas, angry at their neighbors' barking dog…. The list could go on for many pages.

The impact of these feelings upon any healthy engagement with life is like snow poured over flame. Forces of anger, depression, and rage extinguish the qualities of peace and love that are the true birthright of us all. My negative emotions and behaviors spring from a visceral reaction to a world that, in my opinion, fails to give me the love and support I feel that I deserve. In the words of Victor Hugo in this instruction's key quote, I am missing out on the "greatest happiness" because I am convinced that I am not loved.

I become part of this problem especially at those times when I am not doing a good job of loving. An old proverb says that a man who wants friends must show himself friendly. People tend to love loving people. Whenever my heart is overflowing with affection and concern for the people around me, then nothing can make me angry and depressed. Moreover, during those times I realize that I am being loved myself.

Our growing culture of self-absorption underlies a great dysfunction that prevents us from embracing the power that love has to change everything by encouraging me to misinterpret the word "love" so that the focus becomes all about me rather than about the object of my love. The word "cherish" conveys the quality that Victor Hugo was really speaking about. The dictionary says that "cherish" means, "to hold dear, feel or show affection for, to keep or cultivate with care and affection." The cherishing kind of love goes beyond mere emotion and becomes part of my character. Here is a list of characteristics associated with a cherishing kind of love:

> *Love is patient, love is kind. It does not envy, it does not boast,*
> *it is not proud. It is not rude, it is not self-seeking, it is not*
> *easily angered, it keeps no record of wrongs. Love does not*
> *delight in evil but rejoices with the truth. It always protects,*
> *always trusts, always hopes, always perseveres. (1 Cor. 13:4-7)*

To summarize the list: The person who truly loves is one who has learned how to cherish other people.

Of course, some people will certainly not understand, believe, or accept my love. Nevertheless, that's their problem. After all, the Master was crucified by people whom He absolutely loved. My only appropriate goal is to constantly shine the light of sincere love upon the people around me—to provide them with opportunities to spread open the wings of their heart and catch the warmth of love reflected from me if they will. In that way, we can all share together in the "greatest happiness."

# Try This

1. *Surprise somebody who wouldn't expect it from you with a random act of kindness and prepare to experience happiness in their response.*

2. *At least for a few hours deliberately cherish the people around you by expressions of protection, trust, hope, and persistent love.*

# Day 83—Remain Engaged

*Change the changeable, accept the unchangeable, and remove yourself from the unacceptable.* –Denis Waitley

The key quote for this instruction points to three behaviors that facilitate complete engagement with the tasks and relationships belonging to my life. The first two behaviors involve the serious challenge of distinguishing between those things that can actually be changed and those things that are, in fact, unchangeable.

The list of changeable things provides points at which I can transform myself and my world. I could give many examples in which people who are fully engaged in life correct and improve themselves and their circumstances in ways that would never occur to a more withdrawn person—one disassociated with the rhythms of life.

The underlying problem of being disengaged is my willingness at those times to take the less threatening course of action rather than face challenges head-on. As a result, during such times I choose not to accept responsibility for my choices. When fully engaged with life, however, I will go out of my comfort zone and, for example, find the kind of job I could be happy with—being confident that if things didn't work out with the first choice, I would simply try something else.

Acts of engaging whole-heartedly with the processes of my life provide me with the power, energy, and will to make changes to myself and to my environment that I would not otherwise make. My list of the number of things that I feel I am able to change grows longer as I become more engaged with my life. I am in a process of identifying the aggravating and dysfunctional things in my life, and actually changing them—beginning with my own actions and attitudes. This kind of involvement in life is an inseparable part of the growth of character, which the American essayist Joan Didion defined as "the willingness to accept responsibility for one's own life." She further said that such an attitude was "the source from which self-respect springs." Strength of character is the quality that protects us from allowing circumstances to make victims of us.

Emmet Fox, a spiritual leader and one of the founders of Alcoholics Anonymous was one of the many people who took such an attitude even farther in noting the power of the human mind to influence circumstances:

> *The outer world, far from being the prison of circumstances that is commonly supposed to be, has actually no character whatsoever of its own, whether good nor bad. It has only the character that we give to it by our own thinking. It is naturally plastic to our thought, and this is so, whether we know it or not, and whether we wish it or not.*

We can see numerous examples demonstrating the principle. For example, Helen Keller used the unalterable circumstance of being blind and deaf to create a life that changed the world for good.

Accepting of the unchangeable is another important quality that marks the behavior of any person who is fully engaged in life. Peter McWilliams, who wrote a number of self-help books, regards healthy resignation to unalterable circumstance to be of paramount importance, noting that, "Acceptance is such an important commodity, some have called it 'the first law of personal growth.'"

There is a world of difference between the grace of resignation and the defect of fatalism. Through resignation, I will use the circumstance as a source of energy in fashioning an alternate condition in which to continue life. A fatalistic person, on the other hand, will simply bend, or perhaps break, to the circumstance and continue in a diminished life.

Such a vigorous approach to solving the dilemma of whether to change or to accept the world serves to increase my sense of self-assurance, filling me with sufficient confidence to take charge of my life, making changes to improve my situation, altering habits, and making important shifts in my life-style.

# Try This

1. *Think of one changeable part of your life that is causing you aggravation and limiting your enjoyment of life. Plan to take steps to overcome it.*

2. *Identify an unchangeable part of your life that seems to be limiting you. Determine to embrace the thing as part of your own personal growth.*

# Day 84—Engage Completely with Your Life Partner

*If You Hear That a Thousand People Love You*
*remember...saavedra is among them.*
*....*
*AND when you see no one else around you,*
*and you find out*
*that no one loves you anymore,*
*then you will know for certain*
*that...saavedra is dead* –*Guadalupe de Saavedra*

The beautiful poem in this instruction's quote makes me think of my wife. Rae and I have been husband and wife since Richard Nixon's Presidency. People were still alive who had fought as soldiers in the Civil War when we were married.

I remember looking at some old, grainy movies of our wedding day. I saw again how beautiful Rae was then. I recalled how love, admiration, and desire for her were overflowing my heart that day. Those ancient passions are now with me again whenever I think of her. Many times I still find myself really "seeing" Rae—noticing how laughter lights up her eyes; how her features soften when she is thoughtful; how childlike is her delight when she laughs at some witty comment by her grandchild....

The little things provide the greatest joy in our marriage. How often do Rae and I share something together that makes us both throw our heads back and laugh out loud! This shared spontaneous laughter provides some of the cohesion that keeps the two of us bound together. Eric Jong once wrote,

*I know some good marriages—marriages where both people*
*are just trying to get through their days by helping each other,*
*being good to each other.*

My marriage is actually more wonderful than the ones Jong describes, mainly because I am married to a wonderful person. For example, she does a fantastic job of keeping track of our finances (while I, on the other hand, can't even remember what happened to the $60 I had in my pocket three days ago). I don't have enough space to list all the things I could say in praise of my wife:

- Rae keeps our house perfectly—by which I mean permitting

exactly the right amount of clutter.

- She is a servant in her church.
- She is a morally upright person who doesn't demand righteousness of the people around her.
- She is a painstakingly detailed lead copy-editor and bookkeeper for our magazine, and record-keeper for our lives.
- She loves to surprise people by blowing her beloved soap bubbles at unexpected times. (The laughter that sparkles in her eyes as she watches her bubbles is the most perfect expression of the joy of living I ever saw.)
- She is one of the least harmful, most unreflectingly humble people I know.
- She is a blessing to her husband and to her children.

Someone made the comment, "A successful marriage requires falling in love many times, always with the same person." I have learned to "fall in love" with my wife repeatedly. I feel that I am finally at the place where my love for this wonderful person is constant and unvarying. She is what I want. She is what I need. Our shared love is deep and abiding. An ancient proverb describes a faithful wife, and quotes the praise of her husband: "Many women do noble things, but you surpass them all." That's exactly the praise I want to pronounce concerning my wife.

Rae's life is full of people who love her. She constantly reaps the reward of her continual devotion to God; she is the very image of the Old Testament virtuous wife: "Her children arise and call her blessed; her husband also, and he praises her" (Proverbs 31:28)

I put my whole self into life in many ways—none of them more important than my commitment to Rae and to her welfare. I will love her forever.

# Try This

1. *If you are in a relationship, make a list of the things about your partner that you admire.*

2. *For the next 24 hours relate to your partner on the basis of that shining list.*

# Day 85—Manage Your Reflection

*Life is a mirror and will reflect back to the thinker what he thinks into it. –Ernest Holmes*

As the writer and spiritual teacher Ernest Holmes said in the key quote above, life "reflects" back to me the very qualities that I send into the world. The insight has been changing my life. As I come to realize that I am in control of my attitudes, the awareness enables me to alter the course and quality of my life according to my will.

I am conducting a long-term struggle with Esther Hicks' thesis propounded in her monumental *The Secret* philosophy—that each of us is in absolute control over our destiny, whether for good or for evil. According to her, depending upon the "vibrations" that we send out into the Universe, we construct our own reality and therefore live in a heaven or hell of our own making.

Hicks and the multitude of people who ascribe to her philosophy are convinced that she has stumbled upon a true principle by which people can take control of their lives—a principle has led her to make such stirring pronouncements as:

> *Every part of your life has unfolded just right. And so—now—knowing all that you know from where you now stand, now what do you want? The answers are now coming forth to you. Go forth in joy, and get on with it.*

I am not sure if *The Secret* is based upon science or an example of the "pseudo science" that Carl Sagan found so annoying. Nevertheless, I have learned to take whatever good I can from any teaching and to let the rest go. There is a lot of good in Esther Hicks' philosophy.

Hicks would be the first to admit that the dynamic interlocking linkage of perception and reality that she espouses is no recent idea. In *Hamlet*, for example, Shakespeare presented two famous characters—Rosencrantz and Guildenstern—arguing about whether Denmark was a prison. The argument led Hamlet to utter the famous observation, "there is nothing either good or bad, but thinking makes it so."

The drama at that point was powerful because of the fact that Hamlet himself had become imprisoned by his dark thoughts. We might imagine that he uttered the words with wry skepticism because of his inability to cope with his ghastly knowledge that his Uncle Claudius had become both king and stepfather by murdering Hamlet's father. The crime was compounded by his mother Gertrude's duplicity in marrying his father's murderer. The only resolution that Hamlet ever found involved one of literature's most savage dénouements involving the execution of his uncle, the poisoning of his mother, the slaying of his friend, and his own death by both sword and poison.

The heartbreak of Hamlet's "scorched earth" resolution to his dilemma was made even more tragic by the fact that out of his own mouth the words, "there is nothing either good or bad, but thinking makes it so," contained the possible key to his own redemption. Hamlet's principle contained a surmise that might have released him from his dark internal conflicts because his words contained the power to transform the reality of his dark situation by simply negating the ability of the horrible choices of people who were close to him to affect his attitude towards himself and towards his life.

"A million people could be pushing against you, and it would not negatively affect you unless you push back," Esther Hicks wrote:

> *They are affecting what happens in their experience. They are affecting their point of attraction—but it does not affect you unless you push against them.*

This kind of affirmation often becomes true simply because I believe it to be true, whatever actual science it might or might not be based upon. I am sending the reflection of my positive intentions and expectations into the world. As Holms' quote predicted, the universe is reflecting it back to me.

## Try This

1. *Write on a sheet of paper, "I will not permit any situation in my life to pull me down."*

2. *Put the paper on your bathroom mirror or some other place where you will be able to see it often.*

# Day 86—Operate out of Your Passions

*To find fulfillment,...don't exist with life—embrace it.*
*–Jim Beggs*

I don't "embrace life" in the sense that I engage in challenging adventures like bungee jumping or downhill skiing. On the contrary, a chart of my typical daily activities might lead some observers to conclude that I lead a boring or even stodgy existence. Nevertheless, inwardly—in the life awash in the ocean of grace in which I am living these days—I am humming like a plucked piano wire with the sheer joy of being alive.

People who engage in such things as cliff climbing, or hang gliding give the impression of being vibrantly and joyfully alive. However, in some cases the activities are merely attempts to cover the basic emptiness and meaningless of a life with frenetic and even dangerous activities. A respected scientist at an important research facility once made the comment:

> *It's good to have activities in which you become totally immersed. The fact that you have to focus your mind completely on the task at hand is enormously relaxing, because it doesn't allow you to think about any of your problems while you're doing it.*

The gifted and honored scientist was using work as a way of disengaging from life. The unavoidable truth is that any sense that living is worthwhile is an inside job, involving passionate engagement with life. On one hand, some people go on Alaskan cruises or immerse themselves in cutting-edge research to avoid boredom and desperation. On the other hand, people (like me) might eat a baloney sandwich or read a book with every nerve afire with pleasure and gratification.

My attitude of peace and contentment doesn't mean that I never experience sorrow or disappointment. Nevertheless, the spiritual and philosophical foundations of my life are driven into bedrock. Through my faith unlocking God's grace, I have been able to build the house of my life upon a solid foundation. Sorrows and disappointments may shake me up but they no longer can pull me down. I am in good company with my attitude because the Apostle Paul wrote from a dungeon cell:

# How to Put Your Whole Self In

*... I don't have a sense of needing anything personally. I've learned by now to be quite content whatever my circumstances. I'm just as happy with little as with much, with much as with little. I've found the recipe for being happy whether full or hungry, hands full or hands empty (Philippians 4:10-12 The Message Translation).*

A few decades earlier the Roman philosopher Seneca wrote, "Let tears flow of their own accord: their flowing is not inconsistent with inward peace and harmony." A writer named Edith Armstrong drew a compelling word picture to push forward the idea of contentment separated from circumstance:

*I keep the telephone of my mind open to peace, harmony, health, love, and abundance. Then, whenever doubt, anxiety or fear try to call me, they keep getting a busy signal—and soon they'll forget my number.*

The Apostle Paul, Seneca, Edith Armstrong, and I have all found the secret of deriving power for living from day-to-day life. The famous author and medical researcher, Elizabeth Kübler-Ross, made the piercing observation, "There is no need to go to India or anywhere else to find peace. You will find that deep place of silence right in your room, your garden, or even your bathtub."

I am living like that—drinking passionately from reservoirs of wisdom, peace, and fullness so that bad things are powerless to compromise my continual sense of peace and joy. I live so as to find contentment and pleasure in normal things—daily things; all things. I am not existing or surviving in my life; I am embracing it, as Jim Beggs, in this instruction's key quote, says I should. I am continually dazzled by the way in which life keeps hugging back.

## Try This

1. *From now until you go to bed this evening, remain aware of what you are doing, who you are talking to, what is happening to you.*
2. *Engage yourself with passion in each moment as it occurs and observe the dramatic change that will take place in the quality of your life and experience.*

# Day 87—Be Diligent in Your Work

*He who labors diligently need never despair; for all things are accomplished by diligence and labor. —Menander of Athens*

Menander's comment echoes the Bible's wisdom: "Lazy hands make a man poor, but diligent hands bring wealth" (Proverbs 10:4). One of the signs that I am fully engaged in life is that I am accomplishing things that drive the course of my life in directions that are profitable and helpful for myself and for others, while avoiding despair through the "diligence and labor" that Menander spoke about.

Each day's labor becomes a building stone in a growing edifice created by my personal industry. It is necessary for me to be productive because of the demands placed upon me by the fact that I am always writing several books in my ghostwriting business, writing 5-6 articles for my monthly magazine, maintaining a blog, plus writing this book for my motivational speaking business. All of these efforts require diligence and each involves me in a hopeful activity that certainly does protect me from the despair of which Menander wrote. Sigmund Freud taught the role that work plays in making us fully human:

*No other technique for the conduct of life attaches the individual so firmly to reality as laying emphasis on work; for his work at least gives him a secure place in a portion of reality, in the human community.*

I find intense pleasure being diligent about my work because I am doing nothing that I wouldn't do even if it didn't produce income. I derive more genuine pleasure from my work than many people get from going on a vacation. In fact, my work is more pleasant to me than being on vacation myself. Esther Hicks, who wrote *The Law of Attraction*, offered important advice:

*Make a "career" of living a happy life rather than trying to find work that will produce enough income that you can do things with your money that will then make you happy.*

Holding to the attitude towards work and career that Hicks and the others speak about really does protect me against the despair that Menander referred to because there's no possibility of my failing at my work; if I go broke doing something that makes me happy, I haven't really failed. The lost income, in that case, becomes nothing more than a fee paid for my happiness. Market conditions, and disasters are powerless to touch my central core.

On the other hand, it would be a real failure to become wealthy doing something that I hate or find boring. An uncountable number of millionaires are living in despair because they intensely dislike the things they do that earn them their wealth. Dale Carnegie pointed out that, "You never achieve real success unless you like what you are doing." Martin Luther King Jr. proclaimed that, "All labor that uplifts humanity has dignity and importance and should be undertaken with painstaking excellence." Furthermore, he wrote:

> *If a man is called to be a street sweeper, he should sweep streets even as Michelangelo painted, or Beethoven played music, or Shakespeare wrote poetry. He should sweep streets so well that all the hosts of heaven and earth will pause to say, "Here lived a great street sweeper who did his job well."*

I have a sense that I am doing what God or the Universe designed me to do. I am grateful for the grace to strive, as Menander said in the key quote above, to accomplish "all things." To work, as Hicks said, at tasks that make me happy.

# Try This

1. *If you are working at something that doesn't make you happy, look at your occupation from another perspective and focus on the parts of the job that give you satisfaction.*

2. *Identify and fearlessly give yourself to whatever labor will make you completely happy. You will know it when you find it.*

# Day 88—Serve Others

*The true value of a human being is determined primarily
by the measure and the sense in which he has attained to
liberation from the self. –Albert Einstein*

My real answer to the question, "What do you do?" goes deeper than job, profession, and even career. The answer is ultimately spiritual because I am living life in service of others and those acts of service connect me with something greater than myself; they are the way I maintain contact with God.

The life of deliberate service I am living is the way I attain to the "liberation from the self" that Einstein held to be the true measure of value for any person. Commitment to serving others provides the basis for moral excellence and the content for what Einstein, in another quote, declared to be the chief pursuit of any life. "The most important human endeavor," Einstein wrote, "is the striving for morality in our actions. Our inner balance and even our very existence depend on it." He summarized his point by adding, "Only morality in our actions can give beauty and dignity to life."

George Bush Sr. spoke the truth when he wrote, "There can be no definition of a successful life that does not include service to others." Confucius extended the truth by pointing out that, "He who wishes to secure the good of others has already secured his own." Any life cut off from service to others is no life at all. If I ignore those around me, I will be sowing seeds that would grow into a bitter harvest guaranteeing that my life would be an ultimate failure, even if it should end in a palace.

I confirm by practical experience the connection between liberating service for others and personal value and self-worth. Acts of service transform my life from being a jumble of discordant passions, resembling the honking and blatting of instruments tuning up before a concert, into a symphony concert-type performance. Service creates an inner sense of quiet assertion dissipating the dark forces of stress, fatigue, frustration, and dissatisfaction that otherwise prevents me from being truly alive.

In addition, such acts of service provide wellsprings of happiness. One man who knew as much about dedication to helping others as anyone else in his generation observed the fact that, "The only really happy people are those who have learned how to serve" (Dr. Albert Schweitzer). In another passage, Schweitzer wrote: "You must give some time to your fellow men. Even if it's a little thing, do something for others—something for which you get no pay but the privilege of doing it."

My passion for serving others adds a positive redemptive quality to my endeavors. I am like a mason in a stone quarry who believes that he's building a temple rather than cutting a stone. With the good of others in view, I try to do with excellence any task I undertake. "All labor that uplifts humanity has dignity and importance," Martin Luther King, Jr. wrote "and should be undertaken with painstaking excellence."

A principle of the moral universe is that by giving simply, freely, and without reservation, we really do receive more than we can ever give. Service to others freely given *never* feels like sacrifice, because of the joy of service that always accompanies such acts. I will mar the beauty of life by *ever* trying to take anything for myself. There's no place in the moral universe for greed, stinginess, and avarice. I give to others without reserve and then the Universe gives good things back to me.

# Try This

1.  *Within the next week, find some way performing some deliberate act of service—helping in some soup kitchen, perhaps, cleaning trash from some area, or helping meet the need of a shut-in.*

2.  *After it's finished take some time for reflection; take note of the effect that performing the service had about your own attitude towards life and towards the world.*

# Day 89—Practice Temperance

*Use, do not abuse; neither abstinence nor excess ever renders man happy. –Voltaire*

The quality of temperance is not highly rated in the "go for the gusto" world we live in today; we are surrounded by people who are destroying themselves by not being able to control their compulsive behaviors, appetites, and desires. On the other hand, I grew up in a teetotaling environment that regarded a glass of wine as devil's brew. A challenge for each of us in engaging in life is to find the mid-point between enjoying and foregoing the things that are placed in this world for our pleasure.

Four decades ago—long before I had the moral courage to work out the implications of my understanding—I learned that the incidence of alcoholism in Israel is virtually zero, even though families in that country drink wine as a dinner beverage as a matter of course. West Jerusalem or Tel Aviv neighborhoods have bookstores like we have saloons in America. I also learned that the incidence of alcoholism in Salt Lake City—where Mormons teach that you'll be judged by God if you drink a wine cooler—is soaring.

Making rules to forbid drinking alcohol might be an effective way of creating social problems with alcohol. Note, for example, what a failure Prohibition turned out to be. By the end of Prohibition (1933) the per capita consumption of alcohol was higher than before Prohibition was enacted. People were apparently drinking alcohol simply because it was forbidden.

C.S. Lewis observed that God put wine on this earth as a way of blessing us. He also made the piercing insight that, while Islam is a religion of abstinence, Christianity is a religion of temperance. Lewis had no patience for judgmental people and made the observation:

> *An individual Christian may see fit to give up all sorts of things for special reasons—marriage, or meat, or beer, or cinema; but the moment he starts saying the things are bad in themselves, or looking down his nose at other people who do use them, he has taken the wrong turning.*

In my younger days, I spent 12 years as a common laborer and on Friday evenings my fellow workers would sometimes invite me to "stop off" for a beer. I turned them down because of my convictions against any consumption of alcohol, but now wish that I could go back and undo the false standard that prevented me from spending some intimate time with those guys. Some of them were living desperately unhappy lives; I might have been able to encourage them. A schooner of beer might have opened a door through which I could have engaged some of them at a level at which I could have a positive effect on their lives. In fact, some of them were heavy drinkers and I might have provided some support for them with an example of temperance—support that was certainly absent from my hollow and remote goodness.

I am rebuked by the Pharisee's angry denunciation of Jesus Christ because, "He sits with sinners, and drinks with them." If I had the same goal and motivation as Jesus, I would have been a better person if my church-going friends had been able to make the same criticism of me.

Intemperance and abstinence both cut us off from engaging completely in life and in the lives of other people. Overindulgence of anything serves to mar body and spirit and stands as a barrier between myself and the people around me—whether my particular overindulgence involves liquor, food, sodas, Facebook…. The particular arena of compulsive activity doesn't matter at all.

On the other hand, within appropriate constraints anything can become a gateway for engaging in life and in the lives of others in ways that will give me opportunity to express my love for them, and my willingness to serve them in any way possible.

# Try This

1.  *Practice Temperance: Identify one thing in your life that you do to enough excess that it mars your relationship with the people around you or inhibits you from giving your best to tasks you need to do. Keep away from it for the rest of the day, or for the rest of the week, if you can.*

2.  *Indulge yourself in some harmless pleasure or pastime that you have been denying to yourself.*

# Day 90—Let Go of the Wrong Right

*Never does the human soul appear so strong as when it foregoes revenge, and dares forgive an injury. –E. H. Chapin*

When people strike me—whether by fist or tongue—they thereby give me the right to strike back. Eye-for-eye, tit-for-tat, blow-for-blow.... How wonderful it feels when I exercise that right! Only for a brief time, however.

The exaltation that comes from getting the best over another person through any act of vengeance or inappropriate conflict is always fleeting. If I am trying to engage in life, my celebration over the downfall of another will be replaced by remorse; the satisfaction of squashing somebody quickly replaced by emptiness and continued bitterness towards the other person.

Archibald Hart wrote, "Forgiveness is giving up my right to hurt you for hurting me." His quote provides an excellent insight into the nature of forgiveness and redemption. I am becoming a forgiving individual and am instinctively and reflexively giving up my right to strike back at people for whatever harm they do to me. I do this whether or not people deserve my forgiveness. I can't be good for myself and good for heaven's sake unless I am good for those who would be my opponents. I am certainly not good for them when I take out my anger in some act of retribution or some reprisal for any harm that I imagine them to have done to me.

Some people in the past have seriously needed to forgive me and were unwilling to do so. They were willing to exercise their right to harm me—willing to withhold the forgiveness that I needed to receive and that they desperately needed to give. Since coming to awareness of how the moral universe operates, I work diligently to keep things peaceable between me and other people. I am perfectly willing to seek forgiveness for situations that I really didn't create; more interested in establishing peace than in maintaining my honor or showing that I was right.

One test for my humility is how well I handle humiliation that is directed towards myself. "We should mind humiliation less if we were humbler," C.S. Lewis said. So rather than giving in to my initial impulse to strike back at a critic, I'll attempt to learn something from a criticism without trying to judge whether or not the criticism is called-for. After all, I am an unreliable judge of whether a criticism directed against myself is valid because in those situations

# How to Put Your Whole Self In

I am much too prone to give myself the benefit of the doubt.

To the extent I can, I won't strike back even if someone *falsely* accuses me of something. Instead, I'll console myself with the fact that I have done much worse things than whatever they are accusing me of without getting caught. As part of my own coming to humility, I am trying never to be defensive about anything. That starts with my wife, but extends to my entire community of relatives, friends, and acquaintances.

If I ever inadvertently hurt someone's feelings, I try not to defend myself by saying that I didn't mean to offend. Who cares whether I *meant* my remarks to be hurtful? Ignorance is no better than malice when it comes to doing other people harm. The only response appropriate to a humble spirit, in that case, is to say, "I am so sorry I said that. Will you accept my apology?" Then add: "I'll try never to say anything like that again."

My goal is to eliminate hard feelings of any sort towards any person—attempting with as much as in me lies, by the power of God, to conduct every relationship on a level of peace and service.

# Try This

1. *Think of someone who has harmed or offended you in some way and from your heart put away your bad feelings toward that person.*

2. *If possible, commit some kind or generous act for that person as a way of doing your part in healing the division that has come between you two.*

# Day 91—Practice Resignation

*Do not pursue what is illusory—property and position: all that is gained at the expense of your nerves decade after decade and can be confiscated in one fell night. Live with a steady superiority over life—don't be afraid of misfortune, and do not yearn after happiness; it is after all, all the same: the bitter doesn't last forever, and the sweet never fills the cup to overflowing. –Alexander Solzhenitsyn*

I only begin to engage fully in life and in relationship to others as I learn to accept life on its own terms. I can never enjoy myself while desperately wishing my situation to be different than it is. I am living according to Helen Keller's wise admonition, "Keep your face to the sunshine and you will not see the shadows"—a particularly powerful metaphor since it comes from a person who could see neither sun nor shade.

Being resigned to the conditions in my life over which I have no control becomes my pathway to peace—my key to living "with a steady superiority over life," as Solzhenitsyn advised. Unfortunately, people no longer talk about the old virtue of resignation. A sense of resignation to life's circumstances is an essential outcome of my belief in the providence of God. To the extent that I really do accept His control over both circumstances and destiny, I lose my ability to fret and fume because of any trial or difficulty that might arise. The noted devotional writer Oswald Chambers sounded an accurate warning when he wrote:

*We take our circumstances for granted, saying God is in control, but not really believing it. We act as if the things that happen were completely controlled by people.*

Such resignation is different from (and perhaps even the opposite of) fatalism, with which it may be confused. Fatalism reveals itself in such things as an inappropriate passivity concerning the affairs of life. Fatalism, for example, might lead me to regard financial stability as being beyond my control so I fail to be diligent in finding a job or might work in a careless or lazy fashion in whatever job I have. As another example, I might surrender to fate by squandering my resources on lottery tickets.

If I am resigned to the reality of providence, however, then I will try as hard as I can to find a good job and, having found one, will strive to work to the best of my ability. I'll do this because diligence is a characteristic the moral universe calls for me to exhibit. The Bible says, for example, that whatever our hands find to do we should do with all our might and that if we are lazy and unwilling to work we should not eat (2 Thessalonians 3:10).

The will of Heaven will never be something that I simply learn; it must become a process to which I cheerfully submit, because when resigned to the providence of God, I will feel no undo anxiety concerning the outcomes of any efforts. For example, it might not be the will of Heaven that I become financially stable in spite of my best efforts. How blessed would be a life of poverty if a Heavenly Presence accompanies me to the poorhouse! How terrible would be any wealth that would drive that Presence from my life!

Solzhenitsyn's ideals are naturally working themselves out in my life. When completely resigned to the providence of God, of course I never "pursue what is illusory—property and position."

...I obviously am not "afraid of misfortune."

...I naturally do not "yearn after happiness."

Putting aside these negative attitudes and actions frees me to engage completely and with a cheerful mind in all parts of life and makes it possible for me to be strong and helpful in every relationship that I form with every person with whom I come into contact.

# Try This

1. *Consider three things in your life that are troubling you over which you have no control. Put them out of your mind.*

2. *Realize that you are not responsible for outcomes; you are only responsible to do the things that love and duty call for.*

# Day 92—Permit Yourself to Chill

*Once I press myself into action, I immediately begin to live. Anything less is merely existing. The moments I truly live are the moments when I act with my entire will.*
*—Oswald Chambers*

I admit to having a lazy streak. After spending a week aboard a houseboat on the California Delta a few years ago during which I did nothing but read and loaf in the sunshine, I wondered if I am the kind of person who could happily do nothing in particular for the rest of my life. However, I realize that it would be impossible for me to continue perpetually to live in such a state—not because of any innate restiveness, but because something would inevitably attract my passion and draw me back into engagement in life.

My most natural state is to be charged up and throwing myself into an activity with all my will, as Chambers says in the key quote for this instruction, during which I actually accomplish things and reach goals I have set for myself.

I realize during these periods of intense engagement that I really am living life at a different level than while lazing in the sunshine with some piece of escape fiction. On the other hand, during slower periods—those times when I am relaxing or engaged in some pleasant diversion—I don't feel that I am "merely existing," to use Chamber's term. I enjoy reading a good novel, and I love watching movies with my family. I enjoy surfing the Internet or playing card games with my friends and family members.

During these times I still feel perfectly alive. The Bible truthfully says:

> *I know that there is nothing better for men than to be happy and do good while they live. That everyone may eat and drink, and find satisfaction in all his toil—this is the gift of God (Ecclesiastes 3:12).*

Particularly while encountering experiences that might make me anxious or aggravated—such as driving in traffic, for example—can the principle of relaxation exert an especially happy effect. I try to make use of the time spent sitting at traffic lights by singing a merry tune, perhaps. Most of all I can use these periods of enforced inaction for personal silence, which

# How to Put Your Whole Self In

William Penn referred to as being "…to the spirit what sleep is to the body, nourishment and refreshment."

"All work and no play make Jack a dull boy," they used to say. Someone put an edge on the aphorism by noting that all work and no play will make Jill a rich widow."

The advice columnist, Dr. Joyce Brothers, elevated repose into a daily discipline: "No matter how much pressure you feel at work, if you could find ways to relax for at least five minutes every hour, you'd be more productive."

Pleasurable experiences are the frosting on top of the cake of a balanced life. If I throw away the "cake," I certainly will become ill in a very short time. However, on the other hand if I throw away the "frosting" of quiet moments and pleasant activities, I needlessly deny myself appropriate and God-given blessings.

I am grateful for times when I can exert myself and accomplish things for Heaven and for the good of others. However, I am also thankful for pleasant times of relaxation and fun. Both types of experience become satisfying examples of His blessing.

Being able to "chill" sometimes—to just set back on occasion and enjoy life at an easier pace—is a spice that provides good flavoring to the recipe of a balanced life.

# Try This

1. *Assess the way you spent your time during the past several days. Are you taking time to relax and take some pleasure from simply being alive?*

2. *If necessary, set aside some down time in your schedule for tomorrow during which you are going to simply relax while doing something that would provide no measurable profit.*

# Day 93—Live Without Desperation

*The mass of men lead lives of quiet desperation and go to the grave with the song still in them.* –Henry David Thoreau

One of the great things about putting my whole self into life is that I can't remember the last time I had any feelings of desperation. About anything! My willingness to deal with whatever life throws my way stands in contrast to the desperation that, as Thoreau points out, is the common experience of many people. In fact, Thoreau may have been writing about a gentler time than ours, because James Thurber made a witty rejoinder (the key quote for another instruction) that rings true about our own generation: "Nowadays most men lead lives of noisy desperation."

In the great but disturbing movie, *Fight Club*, Tyler Durden (played by Edward Norton) was a young man, living in a lovely condominium, with a high-paying and interesting job. He was bright enough to do anything he wanted and possessed enough money to buy everything he could wish for. Durden was well educated, good-looking, popular, and witty. Nevertheless, within himself he was leading a wretched, desperate existence until a stranger entered his life with a promise of excitement that developed into a stunning reality of mayhem and destruction.

Wealth is small coin when it comes to the price that life demands for genuine satisfaction. Many of us in America have used wealth to hedge our lives about with satiated passions and expensive but useless possessions. Those hedges have grown tall and thick and have moved inward until the light of genuine happiness sometimes become a scarcely visible shadow across the dark recesses into which our spirits have receded.

I read of a desperate family who had $6,500 a month take-home salary, who owned 16 vehicles, including a motor home, who owed $2,000 a month in credit-card debt, and who gave $10 a month to charity. The wife earned $4,000 a month by working 65 hours a week at two jobs, including stocking shelves in a grocery store.

The family imagined that they were devoting themselves to obtaining things that would make their lives pleasant and pleasurable, but found themselves in a horrible nightmare in which possessions were robbing them of the ability to experience joy. Materialism deprives life of meaning and delight.

## How to Put Your Whole Self In

Any desperate striving for wealth and things will divert me from what the Master said were the great issues of life: "justice, mercy and faithfulness." God is waiting to give me the gifts of His presence and His power, but sometimes I have been too distracted by the things in my culture to reflect upon Him and to receive these gifts.

The power to accomplish the required change was observed by Albert Einstein as being rooted in a transformational spiritual experience—which he referred to as "transpersonal."

> *I have yet to meet a single person from our culture, no matter what his or her educational background, IQ, and specific training, who had powerful transpersonal experiences and continues to subscribe to the materialistic monism of Western science.*

The Master put it best when He said, "Watch out! Be on your guard against all kinds of greed; a man's life does not consist in the abundance of his possessions." I am watching out! I am on my guard!

I am grateful that today I am escaping the dark tentacles of our materialistic world. He has opened my eyes to the sunshine of His grace; I am not trying to keep up with anybody. I love my life! I love my home! Life is wonderful!! The Master gives these things to me just for nothing. I am no longer ever desperate! Not about anything!

# Try This

1.  *During the next 24 hours make a fearless assessment of the quality of your life. Focus carefully upon the things you do, the people who you spend time with, and the attitudes you have from one hour to the next.*

2.  *During the same period find at least two people to whom you can "sing" your "song" and with whom you can become vulnerable. Reach out to them in some personal way. Then note the effect it has upon the people and upon yourself.*

# Day 94—Listen for the Footsteps of God

*Anyone can revolt. It is more difficult silently to obey our own inner promptings, and to spend our lives finding sincere and fitting means of expression for our temperament and our gifts.*
*—Georges Rouault*

I have finally learned that I can't engage fully in life by simply talking my way in. The cowboy sage Will Rogers put the idea into its essential form when he said, "Never miss a good chance to shut up." I am trying to develop the habit of not breaking any silence unless I can improve on it. For one thing, silence is a powerful ally for people of limited intelligence. The Bible notes that even a fool who keeps silent is thought to be wise (Proverbs 17:28).

Much of my success in developing positive relationships with others depends upon my ability to control my tongue! My silence in the face of other people's mistakes and failings has become a powerful tool for maintaining quality relationships. I've learned to allow people to be foolish and vain without attempting to correct them because I can depend upon the truth eventually to reveal itself without my assistance. A famous nineteenth century preacher and theologian said:

> *The ambiguous and the false, the unworthy and mean, will ere long overthrow and confute themselves, and therefore the true can afford to be quiet, and finds silence to be its wisdom.*
> *—Spurgeon*

I am also learning to use silence to prevent the debris of my uncensored opinions and reactions from clogging the channels of my interpersonal communication.

Most of all, I am quieting my heart and spirit in order to hear the voice of God; learning to heed to what experience, conscience, and intuition are trying to say to me. An Indian guru, spiritual figure, and educator named Sathya Sai Baba reminds me, "You can hear the footsteps of God when silence reigns in the mind." Only when my inner spirit is quiet can I catch the sound of God's passing and thus follow in the direction that He is going.

For years I've been moved by the story of Elijah the Prophet when he fled into the wilderness to hide in a cave from the wrath of Queen Jezebel who had decided to kill him. As told in 1 Kings 19, Elijah was commanded to stand in the cave's mouth and watch as God passed by. As he stood there, Elijah had a vision of a terrible windstorm that was so fierce it tore apart mountains and crushed rocks. That was followed by an earthquake and then by a fire. But God did not show himself to Elijah in any of those powerful manifestations. Following the shocks of the wind, earthquake, and fire, the Bible says that God came to Elijah in a gentle whisper.

I've had the same experience of going through storms, earthquakes, and fires in my own life but coming to profound understanding only when the turbulence subsided, and I quieted myself enough to catch the soft but unmistakable whisper that denoted His presence.

Shouting at people is never an effective method of communicating with them. I'm learning to gently speak the truth to others in the same reduced volume *sotto voce* that God uses when He quietly speaks His truth to me. Only the practice of appropriate silence makes it possible to obey my own "inner promptings," as Rouault says I must in the key quote above, and to actually search for the means of communication that really is suitable to my gifts and to my essential personality.

# Try This

1. *Reflect on a few instances in which someone said something insulting and demeaning to you. Think of at least one time when you offended someone—perhaps even lost a friend— because of some thoughtless comment.*

2. *Look for an occasion some time during the next 24 hours that will provide you with the opportunity of not making some critical comment, unasked-for explanation, or irritated response that you might otherwise have made.*

# Day 95—Help Yourself

*It is one of the most beautiful compensations of this life that no man can sincerely try to help another without helping himself.*
*–Ralph Waldo Emerson*

I have always been impressed by the gracious attitude of a friend of mine, Jerry. Because whenever called upon to perform a favor, Jerry always leaves the impression with the people he helps that they are the ones doing him a favor by giving him an opportunity to serve. I have decided that Jerry's attitude merely represents his practical recognition of the truth of Emerson's quote.

I have been throwing myself into service, going beyond the Golden Rule of doing for others what you wish them to do for you to the Platinum Rule, which instructs us to do for others what they actually want us to do for them.

The act of genuine service itself provides the greatest source of joy because any generous act has a reciprocating force. People are usually willing to be kind towards someone who has done some good service for them, but that is entirely beside-the-point. The magnificent reality is that acts of service have their own reward. Oprah wrote:

> *I have come to believe that each of us has a personal calling that's as unique as a fingerprint—and that the best way to succeed is to discover what you love and then find a way to offer it to others in the form of service, working hard, and also allowing the energy of the universe to lead you.*

Then Oprah put a beautiful cap on her comment: "The reward of a thing well done is to have done it."

The feelings of satisfaction and pleasure that come from having performed some good deed provide a rich reward, indeed. The great humanitarian, Albert Schweitzer, doubtless spoke from personal experience when he declared, "The only really happy people are those who have learned how to serve."

The beneficial effects of service only come to me as I maintain a selfless attitude towards the deeds I perform. More than 2,000 years ago the Greek philosopher Demosthenes exactly captured the right spirit of service when he wrote:

# How to Put Your Whole Self In

*He who confers a favor should at once forget it, if he is not to show a sordid ungenerous spirit. To remind a man of a kindness conferred and to talk of it, is little different from reproach.*

Some people are unsettled by the prospect of showing unselfish generosity to others out of fear that people will take advantage of them. However, if I love the people around me as God said I should love them, then I want them to take advantage of me. After all, the Bible says: "This is how we know what love is: Jesus Christ laid down his life for us. And we ought to lay down our lives for our brothers" (1 John 3:16).

I believe that if we are too cautious with our boundaries—too careful to ensure that people don't take advantage of us—they will take advantage of us in spite of the walls we erect around our generosity. Our defenses seem to incite them to attack. On the other hand, I have learned that if I deliberately place myself in the service of co-workers, family members, and friends, they do not rush at me to take too much advantage of my kindness. Quite the opposite! They show similar consideration towards me. After all, the Master said: "Give, and it will be given to you. A good measure, pressed down, shaken together and running over, will be poured into your lap" (Luke 6:38).

My experience illustrates the powerful principle that people tend to live up to (or down to) our expectations for them. I expect people to be kind and not impose upon me in some insistent and inappropriate fashion. Therefore, they don't!

I know exactly what is going through my buddy Jerry's mind and heart when it comes to being grateful for opportunities to serve. I am equally grateful for the opportunities that come my way to be of service to others. Emerson was right. I really am helping myself at these times.

## Try This

1. *Each day for the next three days perform some random act of kindness.*

2. *Observe the effect that your generosity produces in your own heart.*

# Day 96—Press On

*Patience and perseverance have a magical effect before which difficulties disappear and obstacles vanish.*
*–John Quincy Adams*

Nobody ever puts him/herself wholeheartedly into any relationship or activity without developing the qualities of patience and perseverance that the sixth president of the United States referred to in this instruction's key quote.

The "magic" that he writes about comes from the cumulative power of small things. A single step is of no consequence. A hundred steps might take you to the corner of the street. A hundred thousand steps will take you across a town. A million steps will carry you to the other side of the planet.

If you faithfully read on a particular topic for a half an hour a day, in 20 years you would have read for a total of 152 days. You would have become a specialist. Accomplishing anything like that would seem magical because patience and persistence work together to unleash a principle noted by Samuel Butler "If we attend continually and promptly to the little that we can do, we shall ere long be surprised to find how little remains that we cannot do."

I have been happily married for over 45 years and a big part of the success of my marriage is getting out of bed in the morning and telling my wife that I love her no matter what my feelings may be. When I married her, I said that I would love her until death parted us, and that was a promise not a prediction.

Some people fail in their marriage because they believe love to be merely an emotion. They no longer feel the emotion and so they break off the relationship. True love, however, is persistent. "Love never fails," the Bible says (1 Corinthians 13:8). Any positive quality in a relationship that ever fails, therefore, was never authentic love.

My success in any job I ever had came to me because when it was time to go to work, I went to work even if I didn't feel like doing so. The only way I could write this book was by whacking away at the keyboard every day whether I felt like writing or not; whether it was convenient for me or not.

The virtues of patience and perseverance operate most strongly in the absence of positive circumstances or emotions. Hope is the quality that carries me through the darkness towards a light that I believe to be at the end of every tunnel even when I am unable to see even a glimmer of it.

The incomparable Ann Lamott wrote the stirring words:

> *Hope begins in the dark,*
> *the stubborn hope that if you just show up*
> *and try to do the right thing,*
> *the dawn will come.*
> *You wait and watch and work.*
> *You don't give up.*

I will certainly fail at any relationship or at any task if I come to believe that my hope is nothing but an emotion. If I stop moving forward when I no longer "feel" hopeful, I'll always quit at anything difficult that I ever do.

President Calvin Coolidge made a brilliantly clear statement of truth when he said:

> *Press on: nothing in the world can take the place of*
> *perseverance. Talent will not; nothing is more common than*
> *unsuccessful men with talent. Genius will not; unrewarded*
> *genius is almost a proverb. Education will not; the world is*
> *full of educated derelicts. Persistence and determination alone*
> *are omnipotent.*

I am pressing on. I'll never stop.

# Try This

1. *Pick out some worthwhile project that you've attempted to start in the past but have been neglecting.*

2. *Make a plan—with whatever charts or schedules are appropriate—to carry the project forward to completion.*

# Day 97—Keep Laughing

*We know that in the human condition, you cannot experience
emotional distress and emotional uplift at the same time.
When you're experiencing mirth, you are not experiencing
depression, anxiety or anger. —Steven Sultanoff*

Part of the challenge of putting my whole self into relationships with others is to maintain control over my emotions and to cultivate the passions that help create the good outcomes in my life and avoid those feelings that only serve to bring me down and to bring down the people that are around me. One of the most effective techniques for doing this involves humor.

Steven Sultanoff, the source of this instruction's key quote, has a PhD and id a self-styled "mirthologist." He believes good humor to be one of the most effective antidotes to the negative emotions that create problems among people.

Sometimes it seems that the darkest moments provide occasion for the best humor. The most unforgettable moment of the show "Roseanne" occurred during a particularly terrible time in their lives. Her husband had been laid off and their economic situation was in desperate shape. They were sitting in their living room when their lights suddenly went out because of non-payment of their utility bill. As they sat there in the ensuing darkness, Roseanne said, "Well, middle class was nice while it lasted."

When my wife's Uncle Jack lost his mother, he and his family were returning from the graveside in a limousine following a second limousine carrying his sister and her family. When both cars stopped at a traffic light, Uncle Jack got out of the car, walked over to his sister's car, and tapped on the window. When she rolled down the window, Uncle Jack asked her in a serious tone of voice, "Pardon me. Have you any Grey Poupon?" The whole car instantly erupted in laughter. Uncle Jack's sister laughed until tears flowed down her cheeks. Later she told him, "Thanks so much, Jack! That was just what we needed!" Milton Berle said, "Laughter is an instant vacation." The fact is that I always found a good laugh to be a great break in any time of pressure or tension.

## How to Put Your Whole Self In

People who are out of touch with the real world are too quick to say the words, "That's no laughing matter" because everything in life is a laughing matter. Of course, we're not talking about laughter involving hurtful emotions such as scorn and derision. However, George Bernard Shaw spoke a profound truth when he said, "Life doesn't cease to become funny when you die any more than it ceases to be serious when you laugh." Appropriate humor becomes a lubricant to grease the wheels of human relationships. I agree wholeheartedly with e.e. cummings' sage comment that "The most wasted of all days is one without laughter." Victor Borge, once observed, "Laughter is the closest distance between two people."

The character of Roger in the movie "Who Framed Roger Rabbit?" was an empty headed ridiculous looking little animal married to a tall, stately, and voluptuous female named Jessica. When someone asked Jessica what she ever saw in Roger, she replied, "He makes me laugh." Humor is one of the great bonds that keep my wife Rae and me in close relationship with each other. I don't think a day goes by without us finding something to laugh at out loud together. Rae has a naturally dry wit and often makes some humorous aside that will absolutely cause us both to burst out laughing. Sultanoff was right in the key quote above that "emotional distress and emotional uplift" cannot exist at the same time. The warm sunshine of appropriate laughter will always melt away the icy grip of "depression, anxiety, or anger."

# Try This

1.  *Watch carefully the conversations you have today and note any witty or humorous comments. What was said? Where was the humor in each incident? What effect did it have?*

2.  *Make sure to engage in some humorous exchange with at least three different people today; notice the effect that good humor exerts on your relationship with them.*

# Day 98—Learn to "Just Deal with it"

*Shut out all of your past except that which will help you weather your tomorrows.* –*Sir William Osler*

The contemporary admonition to "just deal with it!" carries a lot of wisdom. When something dark from my past threatens my sense of peace and harmony, the thing for me to do is simply to take responsibility for my emotions and put that dark thing away from me forever.

Of course, in many cases that's easier said than done. People experience depressions, illness, even insanity because of their inability to successfully cope with awful things that they have experienced, and have done, in their past. I am unable to put myself wholeheartedly into life without coming to terms with my personal history. Such success is powered by the core energy that forgiveness can supply—both as I receive pardon for the things I have done and, in turn, as I pardon others.

I need an attitude adjustment; the winds of grace must cleanse both my unforgiving attitudes and my unforgiven feelings because the two things are powerfully and indivisibly connected with each other. Jesus said that forgiving and forgiveness are two sides of the same coin. "When you stand praying, if you hold anything against anyone, forgive him, so that your Father in heaven may forgive you your sins," He said. Saint Francis reminded us that, "It is in pardoning that we are pardoned." The connection is easy to see; I have to be willing to forgive other people for their errors and wrong-doing or else I couldn't forgive myself for the same things.

Some people are stuck with an unforgiving attitude because of an inability to "shut out" past grievances. Their hearts are filled with anger and bitterness to the point that they regard any pardoning of the person at the center of their wrath as a despicable act. C.S. Lewis hit the nail on the head when he wrote:

*Every one says that forgiveness is a lovely idea, until they have something to forgive.... And then to mention the subject at all is to be greeted with howls of anger. It is not that people think this too high and difficult a virtue: it is that they think it hateful and contemptible.* –*C.S. Lewis*

Such people miss the point that, even though no act of forgiveness can change the past, the smallest act of forgiveness will bless their present and enlarge the future.

I no longer spend a moment worrying about whether people who hurt me deserve to be forgiven because any act of forgiving others is a gift I give myself. I forgive them because anger, bitterness, and resentment are roadblocks that separate me from the qualities of joy, serenity, and the sense of cheerfulness that I want out of life.

The power of forgiveness isn't a religious doctrine; it is a spiritual law. Mercy is "twice blest," Shakespeare said, and then explained how, "…it blesseth him that gives and him that takes…." Buddha agreed, "Holding on to anger is like grasping a hot coal with the intent of throwing it at someone else; you are the one getting burned."

I once read an unforgettable account of the power of forgiveness involving a man named Charlie Hainline, who was a layman at the Coral Ridge Presbyterian Church in Fort Lauderdale. Hainline's daughter was kidnapped and then killed. Her head was found floating in a canal. After his daughter's murderer was convicted, Hainline visited the man in jail in order to offer the man forgiveness.

One day Hainline was with a team that was cold calling people in his church's neighborhood. A teammate was speaking to a man about the need for faith and forgiveness when the person being addressed pointed to Charlie, who had been sitting quietly during the presentation, and said, "If being a Christian would make me like him, I want it!"

Me too! I want the heart that Charlie Hainline has! I want the grace of Heaven to empower me to shut out all of my past except that which will help me weather my tomorrows. And that's just what is happening! Conflict is a regular part of my life, but by the grace of God I am learning to just deal with it.

# Try This

1. *Write on a piece of paper some anger or grievance that you hold in your heart towards another person.*

2. *Completely destroy that piece of paper and embrace the person as an act of deliberate forgiveness.*

# Day 99—Do a Little Bit of Good

*Knowing all truth is less than doing a little bit of good.*
*—Albert Schweitzer*

Putting my whole self into the lives of others is actually an obnoxious and even dysfunctional thing to do unless the act is undertaken with the intention of doing for others those things they need me to do and especially in becoming for them the person they need me to be.

There are many ways in which we can engage deeply in the lives of others without doing them a bit of good. Abusive spouses, controlling mothers-in-law, dominating parents, repressive cult leaders, and infatuated fans are examples of people who engage in an inappropriate fashion in the lives of other people and in every case cause more harm than good. The horrible thing is that in every case the people usually consider themselves to actually be motivated by love for the person they are harming. They are blinded to the fact that they are actually using others as a way of satisfying their own passions and therefore are incapable of doing even a little bit of good.

Infatuation with another person actually eliminates the possibility of engaging with him/her in a helpful way because the focus for any contact is to satisfy the overpowering infatuation rather than to engage in genuine acts of service. Whenever I become infatuated with another person, the relationship is all about me and about satisfying my emotions rather than about the person and meeting his/her actual needs. The object of my attentions may feel flattered but will never feel genuinely served because the service, in that case, can never be offered from a heart moved by genuine concern.

There's a world of difference between someone like Mother Teresa attempting to do a little bit of good for a person dying on a Calcutta Street Corner and a woman trying to give a key to her hotel room to a movie star. The difference in motivations between the two kinds of actions are what cause people in the public eye to grow disdainful of their "adoring public." Mother Teresa is putting her whole self into her relationship with the dying street person; the fan trying to pass her key to the star is feeding her own ego. Similar negative effects, and worse, are created by the other examples— abusive spouses, dominating parents, and repressive cult leaders. The effects of such relationships are always harmful.

# How to Put Your Whole Self In

The intention of simply doing "a little bit of good" is a magnificent motivator for me as I attempt to put my whole self into every relationship in my life. I am not trying to rescue other people. I am not attempting to save people from themselves. I am not trying to set myself up as a shining example for other people to follow. I am just doing whatever little bit of good that comes my way.

The fountains of grace in this world are usually opened up by the smallest of actions. A hug to the person who is a grieving; a warm smile for the harassed woman at the grocery store checkout counter; a simple touch on the arm for a worried parent; a ride to the airport for a single person; a cup of coffee for my wife in the morning when she is doing her hair—these provide the content of my putting my whole self into relationships with the people around me.

I will very infrequently have the opportunity of making some magnificent gesture or sacrifice; I usually put my whole self into other people's lives by the little bit of good that I do for them every day.

# Try This

1. *Today determine to do a little bit of good for every person you encounter without looking for any response from them.*

2. *Avoid doing a single thing for anybody that he/she didn't want you to do.*

# Day 100—Embrace Every Moment with Gusto

*Millions long for immortality who don't know what to do on a rainy Sunday afternoon.* –Susan Ertz

I know what to do on a rainy Sunday afternoon, or any time. Actually, my problem is just the opposite of the one mentioned in this instruction's key quote because of all the things I wish I could do if I only had more time—friends I don't have time to talk with; video games I don't have time to play; TV shows and movies I have no time to watch; books I don't have time to read; Internet sites I wish I had time to visit. Actually, on a rainy Sunday afternoon I would be most likely to get out my laptop and do some work rather than do any of these things. I enjoy the tasks belonging to my profession as much as I enjoy any form of recreation!

There's a better way of living, however, than merely finding ways to keep myself occupied because I can fill my life with light and happiness by doing nothing more than simply waking myself up to the beauty of the world that surrounds me.

Thirteen-year-old Anne Frank, while hiding in an attic from Nazi soldiers who were seeking to put her and her entire family to death, was able to write in her famous journal the amazing words, "Think of all the beauty still left around you and be happy."

The young girl remained cooped up in her little hiding place for more than two years during which time she wasn't able to take trips to visit friends. She had no access to libraries, video games, computers, the Internet, television, or movies. Nevertheless, she apparently knew what it was to be happy with a joy that had its sources in her heart.

Anne Frank's discovery of beauty and happiness in the dark room where she hid 24 hours a day, seven days a week, didn't call for supernatural abilities. Moreover, her ability to experience joy in those wretched circumstances shouldn't come as a surprise. After all, we have always known in our hearts that happiness is where you find it. Following Anne Frank's lead, I ask myself the question. What beautiful things are around me to make me happy? The beauty of the universe and the keys for filling my day with good activities are revealed in Bill Bright's "Ten Rules for Happiness":

## How to Put Your Whole Self In

1. Give something away (no strings attached)
2. Do a kindness (and forget it)
3. Spend a few minutes with the aged (their experience is a priceless guidance)
4. Look intently into the face of a baby (and marvel)
5. Laugh often (it's life's lubricant)
6. Give thanks (a thousand times a day is not enough)
7. Pray (or you will lose the way)
8. Work (with vim and vigor)
9. Plan as though you'll live forever (because you will)
10. Live as though you'll die tomorrow (because you will on some tomorrow)

These are easy rules and are activities that I could engage in on any rainy afternoon. These rules have the power to open me up to beauty. A small girl could do most of them while living in a crowded attic hiding from people who wanted to kill her.

"Happiness is a choice," Adair Lara wrote, "Reach out for it at the moment it appears, like a balloon drifting seaward in a bright blue sky." I am going to grab for it today! It is always, in fact, well within my reach!

# Try This

1. *List three activities in your life that aren't worth getting deeply involved in, and determine to stop doing them.*

2. *Put the Ten Rules for Happiness on a piece of paper and post it somewhere where you can see it often. Fill your mind and heart with those things.*

# Day 101—Prepare to Be Blessed for a Change

*When you change the way you look at things, the things you look at change* —Brian Tracy

Engaging in life with my whole heart has opened my spirit to relish the people and objects around me and to rejoice over the processes of life. I work hard on most days so by bedtime I am usually very tired. Nevertheless, I can't doze off until I have read a few pages from whatever book I am reading at the time. When Mr. Sandman has finally thrown so much grit in my eyes that the words absolutely blur together, I shut off the light, snuggle up to my wife, and often breathe a prayer of thanks that the gift of slumber provides such a perfect remedy for my bone-tired weariness.

I nearly always arise while it is still pitch dark. The routine of morning exercise on my Wii Fit is so much fun that it requires discipline to stop exercising when my half-hour is complete. I take great pleasure from my first cup of coffee and from reading the daily comic strips. Most of them are badly done, in my opinion, but a couple of them are always worth a laugh or two—and five times a week Dilbert is right on.

After 44 years of marriage I still enjoy giving my wife warm hugs at the beginning and ending of each day. Every time I leave her to run an errand I hug her again and we tell each other "I love you." When I return we do it again. Each time it feels good!

My work routines are filled with blessing. Sitting at my computer is my rest state. I never find writing tasks to be boring because whatever particular article or book I am writing at the time often seems to me to be the most interesting thing I have ever written.

My business partner and our sales manager seem to be some of the world's best people; I am delighted to see them every day. They often make me laugh and continually provide reasons why I should admire them even more.

After seven years of being involved in the rhythms of interviewing, writing, conducting reviews, and polishing articles for our *110° Magazine*, I am still continually amazed by the people I encounter and by the extraordinary lives each of them have lived. I come to love every one of them deeply and from my heart. The rhythms of our magazine production remain engaging and satisfying. The process—from choosing the articles to the exciting moment when our first magazines arrive—is continually fascinating.

No words can fully describe the almost magical delights of the progression in the seasons. The colors of fall in Northern California are so beautiful they sometimes make my heart hurt. I begin singing Christmas Carols the day after Halloween. Every spring I find scenes that recall Frost's words, "Earth's first green is gold."

The ultimate cycle of life is that of birth, growth, decline, and death. I am nearing the evening hours of my life; the shadows are lengthening. My autumn has been, by far, the happiest and most productive season of my life.

Some day I will lie down in death. However, I believe that the final rest, when it comes, will be analogous to the blessed sleep that marks the conclusion of each day. I expect in that final sleep to discover an ultimate satisfaction. At that time, with all rhythms and cadences at an end, I hope to experience the sunrise of an Eternal Day.

# Try This

1. *For the next 24 hours engage in the events, tasks, and relationships that come into your life with your whole heart—embracing each of them as sent for the purpose of challenging and blessing you.*

2. *After the 24 hours are up, review the results that followed from your deliberate engagement in the facets of life as they opened up to you.*

WED
1/22/14
CLAYTON-CA

## Motivational Speaker

Dr. Don Huntington is a gifted motivational speaker, able to create positive energies and renewed intentions in any group. His diverse background in technology, business, theology, human relations, and spiritual writing coupled with his sense of humor and unique presentation style make Dr. Huntington a good choice for speaking to any group on any topic having to do with engaging in life on any level.

**Contact Don at**
**don.huntington@gmail.com**
**925-864-3263**
**1822 Periwinkle Way**
**Antioch, CA 94531**